T0132186

AUTOMOTIVE
DEALERSHIP SAFEGUARD
CYBERSECURITY & FINANCIAL COMPLIANCE GUIDE

BRIAN RAMPHAL

authorHOUSE®

AuthorHouse™
1663 Liberty Drive
Bloomington, IN 47403
www.authorhouse.com
Phone: 833-262-8899

Published by AuthorHouse 01/03/2024

ISBN: 979-8-8230-1980-4 (sc)
ISBN: 979-8-8230-1981-1 (hc)
ISBN: 979-8-8230-1982-8 (e)

Library of Congress Control Number: 2023924451

Print information available on the last page.

DEDICATION

To my cherished family, who have been my steadfast anchor. To Chandra, my beloved spouse, your strength and unwavering love are the bedrock of our family.

To my remarkable sons, Keith and Christopher, accomplished technology professionals in their own right. You both have become shining beacons of intelligence, innovation, and integrity.

To my loving and dedicated parents, Chanrowti (Olive) and Pitamber (Ram) Ramphal, who laid the foundation of my hopes and dreams; to my siblings, Gary and Rowena, for our collective heritage and experiences; and to my extended family, whose support was especially notable during my adolescent years.

CONTENTS

AUTOMOTIVE DEALERSHIP: USE CASE

The need for robust cybersecurity measures has never been more pressing in an age when technology drives the automotive industry into new horizons. As the automotive landscape evolves, so do the threats that loom over it. *Automotive Dealership Safeguard: A Comprehensive Guide to Cybersecurity and Financial Compliance,* is a beacon of knowledge guiding us through the intricate maze of challenges that dealerships face in safeguarding their operations and financial integrity.

This book explores the unique challenges automotive dealerships confront daily. It is a testament to their dedication and passion for understanding the industry's complexities and providing practical solutions to the challenges it presents.

The journey through this book is enlightening. It delves deep into the financial regulations that govern the automotive industry, uncovering vulnerabilities that might otherwise remain hidden. It provides a diagnosis and a prescription, offering strategies to fortify data protection and ensure compliance with industry standards.

Importantly, this book recognizes that cybersecurity isn't solely a technological endeavor. It highlights the pivotal role of employee awareness and the delicate balance needed when integrating emerging technologies with stringent security protocols. It reminds us that cybersecurity is a multidimensional challenge that demands an organization's collective vigilance.

As you read further, you'll find insights into the legal frameworks and ISO standards that underpin modern cybersecurity. It advocates for best practices and established frameworks such as NIST, offering a clear path for dealerships to follow as they build their defenses.

But this book isn't just about theory; it's also about action. It equips you with the tools to proactively manage risks, ensuring that your dealership is fortified against known and emerging threats. It empowers you to face the future confidently, knowing you're prepared for the dynamic cyber landscape.

PREFACE

As the automotive industry embraces technology, it becomes imperative to address the growing cybersecurity threats that dealerships face. This guide is a culmination of years of experience, research, and dedication. It offers a road map for dealership owners, managers, and professionals to navigate the complex terrain of cybersecurity and financial compliance.

ACKNOWLEDGMENTS

I extend heartfelt gratitude to the numerous individuals who have contributed to the creation of this guide. Your insights, guidance, and dedication have been invaluable. Special thanks to Gary Ramphal, Rowena Mohabir, Henderson Chatargun, Darryn Persaud, Hasfa Faisal, Chris Blumhagen, Patrick O'Rahilly, Mario Sanchez, Mike Doobay, Duane Okinaka, Dan Woodford, Gust Kouvaris, Les Silver, Jim Roche, Russ Kalchik, Harry Kuo, Albert Chu, Carlos Wang, Steve Greenfield, Suresh Maddula, Sarju (Jai) Persaud, Fred Ramphal, James Persaud, Larry Bruce, Farra Majid, Kevin Winter, Robert Watson, Teddy Ramcharitar, Michael Mohan, Gangaram Singh PhD, Daniel Gibran PhD, Baytoram Ramharack, Gary Tucker, and Fred Van der Neut for their expertise and mentorship.

INTRODUCTION

A. OVERVIEW OF AUTOMOTIVE DEALERSHIPS

Automotive dealerships play a crucial role in the automotive industry, serving as intermediaries between vehicle manufacturers and consumers. Dealerships' extensive networks and expertise facilitate vehicle distribution, sales, and after-sales service. It's not just in the United States; the automotive landscape holds its fort globally. In 2019, the global automotive dealership market size was valued at $245.5 billion and is expected to reach $291.7 billion by 2025.[1] This chapter provides a comprehensive overview of automotive dealerships, highlighting their functions, operations, and significance.

Functions and Operations of Automotive Dealerships

Automotive dealerships perform various functions to ensure the smooth functioning of the industry.

Vehicle Sales

Dealerships are responsible for selling vehicles to consumers. They maintain a diverse inventory of vehicles, including different makes, models, and trim levels, catering to customers' varying needs and preferences. Sales professionals guide customers through the purchasing process, providing information about the features, specifications, and pricing of vehicles. They assist in test drives, negotiate prices, and facilitate financing options.[2]

Vehicle Distribution

Dealerships manage the logistics and distribution of vehicles. They receive vehicle shipments from manufacturers and coordinate the transportation and storage of inventory. Dealerships ensure that the right models

---

[1] https://abdalslam.com/car-dealer-statistics.

[2] https://www.mckinsey.com/industries/automotive-and-assembly/our-insights/as-dramatic-disruption-comes-to-automotive-showrooms-proactive-dealers-can-benefit-greatly#/.

and quantities are available for customers to purchase, optimizing the availability and accessibility of vehicles.

Customer Service

Providing excellent customer service is a core aspect of automotive dealerships. They offer post-sales support, including vehicle maintenance, repair, warranty, and parts replacement. Service departments within dealerships have skilled technicians who perform routine maintenance tasks, diagnose and resolve mechanical issues, and ensure the efficient functioning of vehicles. Dealerships prioritize customer satisfaction by addressing inquiries, resolving concerns, and building long-term relationships.

Financing and Insurance

Many automotive dealerships assist customers with vehicle financing and insurance. They collaborate with financial institutions to offer competitive financing options, helping customers secure loans or lease agreements. Dealerships guide the financial aspects of vehicle ownership, explaining terms, interest rates, and payment schedules. They also facilitate insurance services, helping customers select appropriate coverage options and assisting with the necessary paperwork.[3], [4]

Trade-Ins and Preowned Vehicle Sales

Dealerships facilitate trade-ins, allowing customers to exchange their existing vehicles for new or preowned models. They assess the value of trade-in vehicles based on factors, such as age, condition, and market demand. Dealerships offer fair trade-in values and assist customers in applying the trade-in amount toward purchasing a new vehicle.[5] Additionally, dealerships specialize in selling preowned vehicles, providing customers with a wide selection of reliable and certified used cars.

---

[3] https://www.liveabout.com/a-guide-to-dealership-structure-4082435.
[4] https://www.bankrate.com/loans/auto-loans/dealer-financing/.
[5] https://www.caranddriver.com/auto-loans/a32799402/dealer-options/.

Significance of Automotive Dealerships

Automotive dealerships play a vital role in the automotive industry for several reasons.

Economic Contribution

Dealerships contribute significantly to the economy by generating employment opportunities directly and indirectly. They create jobs in sales, service, finance, administration, and other departments. Moreover, dealerships have a ripple effect on local economies, supporting related businesses, such as auto parts suppliers, repair shops, and advertising agencies.[6] It makes sense since the United States has approximately 17,000 new car dealerships. Further, the nation's 16,773 franchised light-vehicle dealers sold 13.7 million light-duty vehicles in 2021.

Customer Access

Dealerships provide customers with a convenient and accessible platform to explore, compare, and purchase vehicles. They offer a physical location where customers can interact with knowledgeable sales professionals, examine vehicles up close, and take test drives. Dealerships often have extended business hours, making it easier for customers to visit at their convenience.

Product Expertise

Dealership staff possesses in-depth knowledge about the vehicles they sell. They stay updated on the latest models, features, and technological advancements, enabling them to provide accurate and valuable information to customers. Dealerships offer a personalized experience, guiding customers through the vehicle selection process and helping them make informed decisions based on their needs and preferences.

---

[6] https://collegegrad.com/industries/automobile-dealers.

After-Sales Service

Dealerships ensure that customers receive ongoing support even after purchasing a vehicle. Service departments provide maintenance and repair services, ensuring vehicles' optimal performance and longevity. Dealerships honor warranties, address recalls, and assist with any issues or concerns that customers may have, fostering trust and loyalty.

B. IMPORTANCE OF CYBERSECURITY FOR CAR DEALERSHIPS

In today's digital age, the importance of cybersecurity for car dealerships cannot be overstated. As technology advances and businesses become increasingly reliant on digital systems, car dealerships face many risks and threats in the cybersecurity landscape. Dealerships must understand the significance of cybersecurity and take proactive measures to protect their operations, customers, and financial stability.

Risks and Threats Faced by Car Dealerships

Car dealerships are prime targets for cybercriminals due to the valuable customer and financial information they possess. The following risks and threats are prevalent in the automotive industry:

a. Data breaches: Cyberattacks targeting car dealerships aim to gain unauthorized access to databases containing customer information, including personal data and payment details. A data breach can result in severe financial loss, identity theft, and damage to the dealership's reputation.[7]

b. Ransomware attacks: Ransomware is malicious software that encrypts dealership data, rendering it inaccessible until a ransom is paid. Ransomware attacks can disrupt dealership operations, cause financial losses, and damage reputations. Implementing robust backup and recovery systems is crucial to mitigate the impact of such attacks.[8]

---

[7] Smith, J. (2020). "The Growing Threat of Data Breaches in the Automotive Industry." *Journal of Cybersecurity and Information Protection*, 15(2), 45–62.

[8] Johnson, M., and Anderson, K. (2019). "Ransomware Attacks on Car Dealerships: A Comprehensive Analysis." *Journal of Information Security*, 25(3), 87–105.

c. Phishing and social engineering: Cybercriminals employ deceptive tactics, such as phishing emails and social engineering techniques, to trick dealership employees into revealing sensitive information or performing unauthorized actions. Phishing attacks can compromise dealership systems, compromise customer data, and enable further cyber threats. Employee training and awareness programs are essential to combat these threats effectively.[9]

d. Malware and viruses: dealership systems can be infected with malware and viruses, leading to data loss, system crashes, and unauthorized access. Malicious software can be spread through various channels, including malicious web sites, infected email attachments, or compromised network connections. Critical preventive measures include regular technology infrastructure hardware and software scanning, updating security software, and implementing firewalls.[10]

Consequences of Cybersecurity Breaches

Protecting Reputation

A cybersecurity breach can have a devastating impact on a dealership's reputation. When customer data is compromised or unauthorized access occurs, trust and confidence in the dealership's ability to protect sensitive information is eroded. News of a breach can quickly spread, leading to negative publicity, damaging the dealership's reputation among current and potential customers, and resulting in a loss of business opportunities. By prioritizing cybersecurity, dealerships can demonstrate their commitment to data protection, maintain a positive brand image, and preserve their hard-earned reputation.

Safeguarding Customer Trust

Customers entrust their personal information to car dealerships during the vehicle purchase process. It includes financial details, credit card information, and personally identifiable information. Cybersecurity

---

[9] Brown, A., and Thompson, L. (2018). "Phishing Attacks on Car Dealerships: Prevention Strategies and Case Studies." *International Journal of Cybersecurity Research*, 10(4), 123–141.
[10] White, T., and Davis, R. (2019). "Malware and Virus Protection in Car Dealerships: Best Practices and Case Studies." *Journal of Cybersecurity*, 20(1), 56–72.

breaches can result in the exposure of this sensitive data, leading to identity theft, financial fraud, and other harmful consequences for customers. By implementing robust cybersecurity measures, such as encryption, access controls, and secure payment processing systems, dealerships can instill confidence in their customers that their data is safe and protected. It fosters trust, strengthens customer relationships, and encourages repeat business.

Ensuring Regulatory Compliance

Car dealerships are subject to various regulations and compliance standards related to data privacy and security. For example, the General Data Protection Regulation (GDPR) in the European Union and the California Consumer Privacy Act (CCPA) in the United States impose strict requirements on how customer data is collected, stored, and processed. Noncompliance with these regulations can result in significant financial penalties and legal consequences. By prioritizing cybersecurity, dealerships can ensure compliance with relevant laws, protecting themselves from legal risks and reputational damage.

Mitigating Financial Losses

Cybersecurity breaches can have severe financial implications for car dealerships. Apart from the costs associated with investigating and remediating the breach, dealerships may face financial losses due to theft of funds, fraudulent transactions, or business disruption. Furthermore, customers affected by a breach may seek compensation for damages. By investing in cybersecurity measures, such as firewalls, intrusion detection systems, and employee training, dealerships can reduce the risk of cyber incidents, minimize financial losses, and maintain financial stability.

Enhancing Business Continuity

Cybersecurity incidents like ransomware attacks or network disruptions can disrupt dealership operations and lead to significant downtime. It can result in a loss of productivity, revenue, and customer satisfaction. Dealerships can enhance their business continuity capabilities by implementing robust cybersecurity protocols, including regular data backups, disaster recovery plans, and incident response procedures. It ensures that operations can be quickly restored despite a cyberattack, minimizing the impact on the dealership's overall performance.

Gaining Competitive Advantage

In a competitive automotive market, cybersecurity can be a key differentiator for dealerships. Customers are increasingly concerned about the security of their personal information and are more likely to choose businesses that prioritize cybersecurity. By implementing robust security measures, dealerships can position themselves as trusted entities prioritizing customer data protection. Further, it can attract security-conscious customers, differentiate the dealership from competitors, and ultimately increase customer loyalty and market share.

The Evolving Automotive Industry and Cybersecurity Risks

The automotive industry's rapid evolution has brought tremendous vehicle capabilities and connectivity advancements. However, with these innovations come new security threats that cybercriminals exploit to target dealerships and their customers. As vehicles become more advanced, cybercriminals find new entry points and attack vectors to compromise the ecosystem.

Latest Trends and Tactics in Phishing Attacks

One of the top cybersecurity threats facing car dealerships is phishing attacks. These attacks involve cybercriminals using deceptive techniques to impersonate legitimate entities and trick dealership employees and customers into revealing sensitive information. Recent trends in phishing attacks include the emergence of smishing (SMS phishing) and vishing (voice phishing), whereby attackers use text messages or phone calls to deceive targets. The use of artificial intelligence to create deepfake voices has added a new layer of sophistication to vishing attacks, making them even harder to detect.

Like many entities, car dealerships are prime targets for these deceptive tactics. Phishing attacks involve cybercriminals masquerading as legitimate entities to manipulate dealership staff and customers into divulging sensitive information. As the digital landscape evolves, so do the tactics employed by cybercriminals. In this ever-evolving cyber battlefield, staying abreast of the latest trends and tactics in phishing attacks is crucial.

Smishing and Vishing

Recently, the realm of phishing attacks has expanded to encompass new avenues of deception—smishing and vishing. Smishing, an amalgamation of "SMS" and "phishing," involves attackers sending fraudulent text messages to victims. These messages often contain enticing offers or alarming warnings, enticing recipients to click on malicious links or reveal personal information. Similarly, vishing, or voice phishing, takes advantage of the human tendency to trust auditory information. Attackers use phone calls to impersonate trusted entities, such as banks or government agencies, and manipulate recipients into divulging confidential data.

Adding a new layer of complexity to vishing attacks is the integration of artificial intelligence (AI). With the advent of deep learning and AI, cybercriminals can create convincing deep fake voices that mimic trusted individuals' tones, cadence, and nuances. This technology enables attackers to craft incredibly realistic phone calls, making it even more challenging for targets to discern fraudulent intent.

Deep Voice Faking: The AI-Powered Threat

The emergence of AI-driven deep fake voices has ushered in a new era of sophistication in vishing attacks. These malicious actors harness AI algorithms to replicate the voices of legitimate dealership staff, executives, or authoritative figures. The result is an eerily accurate imitation that can deceive even the most discerning ear. This technology enables attackers to manipulate emotions, create a sense of urgency, and convince recipients to take actions that compromise security.

Imagine a dealership executive receiving a call from a seemingly credible source within the dealership urgently requesting access to sensitive customer data. The AI-generated voice is so convincing that the executive doesn't question the request's legitimacy, leading to a breach of confidential information. This convergence of AI and vishing amplifies the need for robust security measures and employee awareness to counteract these evolving threats.

Strengthening Defenses

Knowledge is the ultimate weapon against phishing attacks in this fast-evolving cybersecurity landscape. Recognizing the tactics of smishing and vishing and understanding the potential impact of AI-driven deep fake voices is paramount. Car dealerships must proactively educate their staff and customers about these evolving threats and emphasize the importance of vigilance.

Regular cybersecurity training should include smishing and vishing attack simulations, helping employees recognize the telltale signs of deception. By encouraging employees to verify requests independently, dealerships can create an additional layer of defense against these intricate tactics.

Compliance with Government Agencies and Financial Regulations

Car dealerships must comply with various US government agency regulations and financial laws to safeguard customer data and ensure transparent communication. The Fair Credit Reporting Act (FCRA) requires compliance when using consumer credit information, protecting consumers from potential misuse. The Truth in Lending Act (TILA) mandates clear communication of loan terms to consumers, ensuring they understand their financial commitments. The Gramm-Leach-Bliley Act (GLBA) focuses on explaining information-sharing practices, safeguarding sensitive data, and maintaining customer privacy and trust.

C. BRIEF OVERVIEW OF THE MAIN CYBERSECURITY THREATS

Car dealerships face a multitude of cybersecurity threats in today's digital landscape. Understanding these threats is crucial for developing effective security strategies and protecting dealership assets. This section explains the leading cybersecurity threats targeting car dealerships, including common attacks, such as phishing, ransomware, data breaches, insider threats, third-party risks, and social engineering attacks. Dealerships can better assess their risks and implement appropriate security measures by comprehensively understanding these threats.

Phishing Attacks

Phishing attacks are one of car dealerships' most prevalent and persistent threats. According to a report by *Security Magazine,* 15 percent of car dealers have experienced a cybersecurity incident in the past year. Of those impacted, 85 percent of the occurrences were due to sophisticated phishing attempts concealed as legitimate emails that resulted in data breaches, IT-related business interruptions, and loss of revenue. In a phishing attack, cybercriminals impersonate legitimate entities to trick dealership employees or customers into divulging sensitive information, such as login credentials or financial details. These attacks are typically carried out through deceptive emails, malicious web sites, or phone calls. The consequences of successful phishing attacks can be severe, including unauthorized access to systems, data breaches, and financial losses.

Ransomware Attacks

Ransomware poses a significant threat to car dealerships, with potentially devastating consequences. Ransomware is malware that encrypts critical data and demands a ransom payment in exchange for the decryption key. When a dealership's systems are infected with ransomware, it can lead to operational disruptions, loss of customer data, and financial losses. Recovery from ransomware attacks can be time-consuming and expensive, emphasizing the importance of robust preventive measures.

Data Breaches

Data breaches can have severe consequences for car dealerships and their customers. A data breach occurs when unauthorized individuals gain access to sensitive information, such as customer data, financial records, or employee details. The stolen data can be used for various malicious purposes, including identity theft, financial fraud, or resale on the dark web. Data breaches result in financial losses, erode customer trust, and expose the dealership to legal and regulatory consequences.

Insider Threats

Insider threats refer to cybersecurity risks originating from within the dealership itself. These threats can come from employees, contractors, or individuals with authorized access to dealership systems and information. Insider threats can involve unauthorized access, data theft, sabotage, or the inadvertent disclosure of sensitive information. Detecting and mitigating insider threats requires robust access controls, monitoring systems, and employee awareness programs.

Third-Party Risks

Car dealerships often collaborate with third-party vendors, partners, and service providers, introducing additional cybersecurity risks. If these third parties have weak security practices or suffer a breach, the dealership's systems and data could be compromised. Managing third-party risks involves conducting due diligence assessments, implementing contractual safeguards, and monitoring security practices.

Social Engineering Attacks

Social engineering attacks exploit human psychology to manipulate individuals into revealing sensitive information or performing actions that benefit the attackers. Car dealerships are vulnerable to social engineering techniques such as pretexting, baiting, or impersonation. These attacks often target employees, aiming to bypass security controls or gain access to sensitive systems or data. Educating employees about social engineering tactics and implementing vital security awareness programs are essential countermeasures.

Automotive cybersecurity is rapidly evolving, and car dealerships must stay informed about emerging threats and security best practices. By recognizing and understanding these primary cybersecurity threats, car dealerships can develop comprehensive security strategies to mitigate risks effectively. Implementing preventive measures, such as robust email filters, employee training, multifactor authentication, network segmentation, intrusion detection systems, and encryption protocols, can help defend against these threats. Regular vulnerability assessments, penetration testing, and incident response exercises enable dealerships to identify weaknesses and respond effectively to potential cybersecurity incidents. By staying vigilant and proactive, car dealerships can enhance their cybersecurity posture and protect their operations, customers, and reputation from these evolving threats.

Real-Life Examples of Phishing Attacks on Car Dealerships

To underscore the importance of proactive measures, real-life case studies of phishing attacks on car dealerships highlight the devastating impact such attacks can have. Toyota Boshoku Corporation fell victim to a social engineering and Business Email Compromise (BEC) attack, resulting in a loss of $37 million due to wire transfer fraud. Info-stealer campaigns targeting German car dealerships and manufacturers revealed the deployment of info-stealing malware, emphasizing the need for robust cybersecurity infrastructure. Throughout the guide, we will share real-life case studies and examples to elevate the importance of cybersecurity in the automotive sector.

CHAPTER 1

UNDERSTANDING THE CYBERSECURITY LANDSCAPE IN THE AUTOMOTIVE INDUSTRY

A. CURRENT TRENDS AND CHALLENGES IN AUTOMOTIVE CYBERSECURITY

The automotive industry is undergoing a digital revolution with vehicles becoming more connected and technologically advanced. However, this rapid evolution brings unique cybersecurity challenges requiring careful attention and proactive measures.[11] Let's examine the current trends and challenges in automotive cybersecurity.

Massive Scale and Density

The automotive industry operates on a massive scale, with millions of vehicles on the road. Each vehicle is a complex network of electronic control units (ECUs) that perform various functions. Managing cybersecurity risks for such a vast and densely packed IT infrastructure is a significant challenge. Car manufacturers address this challenge by incorporating cybersecurity measures into the design and manufacturing stage, embedding security features into vehicle parts.[12]

Regulations Requiring Cybersecurity Type Approval

Unlike the IT industry, where cybersecurity responsibilities primarily lie with users, the automotive industry holds original equipment manufacturers (OEMs) directly accountable for cybersecurity. Governments have established regulations such as UNECE's WP.29 working party mandating vehicular cybersecurity-type approval. In other words, all vehicles must undergo assessment and qualification before being sold, ensuring they meet cybersecurity standards.[13]

System Complexity

The internal system of a vehicle, known as the electrical and electronic (E/E) architecture, is highly complex. It consists of numerous hardware components and over 100 ECUs, all working to ensure a car's functionality.

---

[11] https://www.mckinsey.com/industries/automotive-and-assembly/our-insights/cybersecurity-in-automotive-mastering-the-challenge.

[12] https://autocrypt.io/top-6-cybersecurity-challenges-automotive-industry/.

[13] https://www.mckinsey.com/industries/automotive-and-assembly/our-insights/cybersecurity-in-automotive-mastering-the-challenge.

Securing the entire system is daunting, with millions of lines of code and various ECUs serving unique purposes. Collaboration between OEMs, cybersecurity providers, and ECU manufacturers is necessary to implement cybersecurity measures effectively.[14]

Long Life Span

Vehicles have a longer life span compared to electronic devices. As consumers keep their cars for extended periods, OEMs face the challenge of managing software updates and addressing security vulnerabilities throughout a car's lifecycle. The increasing number of active vehicles on the road also strains Vehicle Security Operation Centers (vSOCs) responsible for real-time monitoring and threat response.

Scattered Locations

Unlike traditional enterprise networks, vehicles constantly move, traversing cities and countries. This poses challenges for vSOCs as vehicles may enter areas with limited or no internet connectivity, hindering timely threat detection and response. Robust mechanisms are needed to ensure effective monitoring and protection across various locations.

Damage Severity and Recovery

A successful cyberattack on a vehicle system compromises data and poses a risk to passenger safety and public security. Recovering from such attacks and patching vulnerabilities is more complex in the automotive industry. Collaboration between OEMs, Tier 1 suppliers, and cybersecurity providers is essential to ensure seamless updates and mitigate risks effectively.

Automotive Cybersecurity Vulnerabilities

The automotive industry is rapidly evolving, with manufacturers continuously expanding vehicle capabilities and connectivity. However, along with new technologies, there also come new security threats. As vehicles become more advanced, the number of vulnerabilities and attack

---

[14] https://autocrypt.io/top-6-cybersecurity-challenges-automotive-industry/.

vectors that adversaries can exploit increases, posing risks to various sectors of the automotive ecosystem.

Vehicle Vulnerabilities

A cyberattack on a vehicle can have catastrophic consequences, as attackers target various areas, including the following:

- Vehicle safety: Adversaries can gain control over a vehicle's functions, such as fully remote starting or stopping the engine, potentially endangering the occupants.
- Vehicle security: With the increasing use of remote lock systems, attackers can exploit vulnerabilities and gain unauthorized access to a vehicle.
- Vehicle tracking: Cybercriminals can exploit GPS technology to retrieve the location of a vehicle, compromising privacy and potentially facilitating theft or surveillance.[15]
- Data protection: Attackers can remotely take over accounts through email phishing or other methods, compromising customer data, including personal information, such as full names, phone numbers, email addresses, and home addresses.

These are just a few examples of connected vehicles' vulnerabilities, highlighting the critical importance of robust cybersecurity measures.

Business System Vulnerabilities

Adversaries can also target business systems within automotive dealerships, causing significant disruptions to operations. Some of the prevalent types of attacks on the automotive industry include the following:

Ransomware: Attackers deploy malware that encrypts sensitive data, demanding a ransom payment for the decryption key. Failure to comply may result in the public release of stolen data or prolonged disruption of dealership operations.

Data breaches: Security breaches involving unauthorized access to sensitive or confidential data can be highly costly for a dealership. Financial penalties can be issued under data protection regulations, such as the

---

[15] https://eandt.theiet.org/content/articles/2023/05/is-your-car-safe-from-a-cyber-attack/.

California Consumer Privacy Act and other states privacy act, if sensitive data is compromised.

Distributed denial of service (DDoS): Adversaries initiate DDoS attacks to flood web resources, overwhelming the dealership's online operations and denying access to legitimate users.[16]

B. ANALYSIS OF CYBERSECURITY RISKS SPECIFIC TO CAR DEALERSHIPS

Car dealerships face unique cybersecurity risks that require careful analysis and proactive risk mitigation strategies. Further, the auto industry could face particularly significant dangers in 2024. Attacks in the automotive space can impact automakers, automotive fleets, and consumers alike. Reducing these risks will be crucial as more cybercriminals seek to capitalize on the sector's vulnerabilities.[17] Understanding the potential entry points for cyberattacks is critical in implementing effective security measures. The following areas represent significant cybersecurity risks specific to car dealerships:

Dealership Data Management Systems

Car dealerships handle vast customer data, including personal information, financial records, and vehicle purchase history. This makes customer data management systems an attractive target for cybercriminals. A breach in these systems can result in unauthorized access, theft, or misuse of sensitive customer information, leading to reputational damage, legal consequences, and financial losses.[18]

Financial Transactions

Car dealerships process many financial transactions, including vehicle sales, financing, and leasing. This financial data, such as credit card information and banking details, is valuable to cybercriminals seeking to commit fraud. Breaches in financial transaction systems can lead to financial losses, identity theft, and damage to customer trust.

---

[16] https://link.springer.com/article/10.1007/s42154-021-00140-6.

[17] https://www.tripwire.com/state-of-security/auto-industry-higher-risk-cyberattacks.

[18] https://dealersocket.com/products/crm/.

Internal Networks

The internal network infrastructure of car dealerships, including servers, workstations, and other infrastructure-connected devices, represents another potential entry point for cyberattacks. Weak network security practices, outdated software, unpatched vulnerabilities, or insufficient access controls can expose the dealership's internal systems to threats like malware infections, unauthorized access, or privilege escalation.

Third-Party Integrations

Car dealerships often integrate with third-party vendors, suppliers, and service providers to streamline operations and enhance customer experiences. However, these integrations introduce additional cybersecurity risks. If a third party has inadequate security measures, it can be a gateway for attackers to gain unauthorized access to the dealership's systems or data. Due diligence in vetting and monitoring third-party vendors is crucial to mitigate these risks.

Employee Awareness and Training

Employees play a critical role in maintaining cybersecurity within car dealerships. Lack of cybersecurity awareness among employees can lead to accidental actions that compromise security, such as falling for phishing emails or sharing sensitive information. Implementing comprehensive cybersecurity training programs and promoting a culture of security awareness can significantly reduce the risk of human error-related incidents.[19]

Mitigation Strategies

Implement Robust Access Controls

Limit access privileges to sensitive systems and data based on the principle of least privilege. The principle of least privilege advocates granting individuals or processes only the minimum necessary access rights to perform their tasks. This reduces the potential impact of security breaches by limiting unnecessary

---

[19] https://digitaldealer.com/dealer-ops-leadership/four-cybersecurity-basics-must-haves-auto-dealerships/.

permissions and should be regularly reviewed to ensure access remains aligned with job roles. It's a core tenet of cybersecurity to minimize risks from unauthorized access. Regularly review and update access permissions to ensure only authorized individuals can access critical resources.

Encrypt Data

Use encryption techniques to protect sensitive data at rest and in transit. Encryption provides an additional layer of security, even if unauthorized individuals gain access to the data. A report from Airiam highlights that the revised rule provides updated, concrete guidance for businesses and requires companies covered by the rule to implement essential security measures to keep customer data secure.[20]

Implement Strong Authentication

Implement multifactor authentication (MFA) for systems and applications to enhance authentication security. MFA adds an extra layer of protection by requiring users to provide multiple pieces of evidence to verify their identity.

Regularly Update and Patch Systems

Keep software, operating systems, and firmware up to date with the latest security patches. Regularly apply security updates to mitigate vulnerabilities that cybercriminals may exploit.

Conduct Regular Security Audits and Penetration Testing

Regularly assess the dealership's security posture through audits and penetration testing. These proactive measures help identify vulnerabilities and weaknesses that must be addressed promptly.

Establish Incident Response and Recovery Plans

Develop and regularly test incident response and recovery plans to ensure a timely and effective response to cybersecurity incidents. It includes

---

[20] https://airiam.com/auto-dealerships-cybersecurity/.

establishing procedures for containing and mitigating attacks, notifying affected parties, and restoring systems and data.

C. IMPLICATIONS OF CYBERATTACKS ON DEALERSHIP OPERATIONS AND CUSTOMER TRUST

Cybersecurity breaches can have far-reaching implications for car dealerships, impacting their operations and customer trust. Examining the potential consequences of successful cyber incidents is essential for dealerships to comprehend the urgency of prioritizing robust cybersecurity measures.

Disruption of Dealership Operations

A cyberattack can cause significant disruptions to critical dealership operations. Ransomware attacks, for instance, can encrypt essential data and systems, making them inaccessible until a ransom is paid or the data is recovered. Such disruptions can result in extensive downtime, affecting vehicle sales, customer service, and overall business productivity. The financial impact of operational disruptions can be substantial, leading to potential revenue losses and additional recovery costs.

Financial Losses

Cyberattacks can result in financial losses for car dealerships through various avenues. Apart from the potential revenue loss caused by operational disruptions, dealerships may face direct financial extortion through ransom demands. Additionally, cyber incidents can lead to legal expenses, regulatory fines, and compensation costs related to data breaches or compromised customer data. The financial ramifications of cybersecurity breaches can be significant and long-lasting.

Compromised Customer Data

Car dealerships store vast amounts of sensitive customer data, including personal and financial information. A successful cyberattack can expose this data to unauthorized access and theft, compromising the privacy and security of customers. The theft of customer data can lead to identity theft, financial fraud, and other cybercrimes, negatively impacting the affected customers and eroding their trust in the dealership. Rebuilding customer trust after a cybersecurity breach can be challenging and time-consuming.

Damage to Reputation and Customer Trust

Cybersecurity incidents can have a severe impact on a dealership's reputation. News of a cyberattack or data breach can spread quickly, leading to negative media coverage and public scrutiny. Customers may lose trust in the dealership's ability to protect their data and may be hesitant to conduct business with a dealership that has experienced a cyber incident. The damage to reputation can lead to decreased customer loyalty, diminished sales, and potential loss of business partnerships.

Legal and Regulatory Consequences

Car dealerships are subject to various data protection and privacy regulations, and a cybersecurity breach can lead to legal and regulatory consequences. Depending on the jurisdiction, dealerships may face fines, penalties, and legal actions from affected customers or regulatory authorities for failing to protect customer data adequately. Compliance with data protection regulations is crucial to avoid legal liabilities.

Potential Legal Liability

In cases where customer data is compromised, car dealerships may face legal liability for any resulting damages. Customers whose data has been exposed in a breach may seek compensation for financial losses, emotional distress, and other damages resulting from the incident. Legal battles can be time-consuming and costly, further adding to the financial burden on the dealership.

Potential Implications

Invest in Robust Cybersecurity Measures

Implement comprehensive cybersecurity measures, including firewalls, intrusion detection systems, encryption, and multifactor authentication, to protect against cyber threats and potential data breaches.

Conduct Regular Security Training

Educate employees about cybersecurity best practices, including recognizing phishing attempts and practicing secure data handling. Well-informed employees are the frontline defense against cyber threats.

Implement Incident Response Plans

Develop and regularly test incident response plans to ensure a swift and effective response to cyber incidents, minimizing their impact and facilitating faster recovery.

Maintain Data Backups

Regularly back up critical data and systems to ensure quick recovery in case of ransomware attacks or data breaches. Backups are essential to restore operations with minimal disruption.

Comply with Data Protection Regulations

Ensure compliance with relevant data protection and privacy regulations to avoid legal and regulatory consequences. Staying up to date with evolving regulations is critical to maintaining legal compliance.

CHAPTER 2

PHISHING ATTACKS: THE TOP CYBERSECURITY THREAT TARGETING CAR DEALERSHIPS

A. DEFINITION AND EXPLANATION OF PHISHING ATTACKS

Phishing attacks are among the most prevalent and dangerous cyber threats car dealerships face today. This section will comprehensively define phishing attacks and shed light on their objectives. Additionally, we will explore how cybercriminals utilize deceptive techniques to trick dealership employees and customers into revealing sensitive information.

These attacks are a form of social engineering cyberattacks where malicious actors impersonate legitimate entities or individuals to deceive victims into divulging sensitive information, such as login credentials, financial details, or personal data. These attacks are typically conducted through deceptive emails, fraudulent web sites, or even phone calls aiming to exploit human vulnerabilities and trust.[21]

Objectives of Phishing Attacks

- Data theft: Cybercriminals aim to steal sensitive and confidential information from dealership databases, including customer records, financial data, and employee credentials. Once obtained, this information can be used for identity theft, financial fraud, or even sold on the dark web for monetary gain.
- Financial gain: Phishing attacks often target individuals who have access to dealership financial systems or conduct financial transactions on behalf of the business. By gaining unauthorized access to such accounts, attackers can manipulate financial operations, transfer funds, or engage in fraudulent activities, resulting in financial losses for the dealership.
- Business disruption: Some phishing attacks may aim to disrupt dealership operations by infecting the dealership computer network, email, and other software systems with malware or ransomware. This can lead to operational downtime, hampering vehicle sales, customer service, and overall business productivity, ultimately impacting revenue and customer satisfaction.[22]

---

[21] https://www.cisco.com/c/en_in/products/security/email-security/what-is-phishing.html.
[22] https://en.wikipedia.org/wiki/Phishing.

The Impact of Phishing Attacks on Car Dealerships

The information shared in the *2022 State of Cybersecurity in the Dealership report* highlights the severity of the threat posed by phishing attacks on the automotive industry. The survey findings indicate that 85 percent of cybersecurity incidents experienced by car dealerships resulted from sophisticated phishing attempts. These attacks have led to data breaches, business interruptions, and financial losses, highlighting the urgency for dealerships to address this cybersecurity threat.[23]

To combat phishing attacks effectively, car dealerships should adopt robust cybersecurity measures, including the following:

- Email security: Implement advanced email security solutions to detect and block phishing emails before they reach employees' inboxes. This includes spam filters, malware scanners, and link analysis tools.
- Employee training: Conduct regular cybersecurity awareness training for all dealership staff, educating them on how to recognize phishing attempts, avoid clicking on suspicious links, and report potential phishing emails.[24]
- Multifactor authentication: Enable MFA for all dealership accounts to add an extra layer of security, making it more challenging for attackers to gain unauthorized access even if login credentials are compromised.
- Web security: Deploy web filtering and URL reputation services to prevent employees from accessing known malicious web sites and phishing pages.
- Incident response plan: Develop a comprehensive incident response plan to swiftly respond to and mitigate the impact of phishing attacks, minimizing potential data breaches and operational disruptions.

By prioritizing cybersecurity infrastructure upgrades, enhancing employee awareness, and investing in expert cybersecurity personnel, car dealerships can proactively defend against phishing attacks and bolster their

[23] https://www.securitymagazine.com/articles/98487-phishing-is-the-top-cybersecurity-threat-targeting-car-dealerships.
[24] https://www.cdkglobal.com/sites/cdk4/files/PDFfiles/22-4000%20State%20of%20Cybersecurity%202022_Ebook_V9.pdf.

cybersecurity posture. Taking proactive measures is crucial in safeguarding dealership operations, protecting customer data, and maintaining the trust of their clients amid the ever-evolving landscape of cyber threats.

B. TACTICS AND TECHNIQUES USED BY CYBERCRIMINALS

Phishing attacks are successful due to cybercriminals' sophisticated tactics and techniques to deceive and manipulate dealership employees and customers. This section will delve into the various strategies malicious actors use in phishing attacks, focusing on social engineering methods that exploit human vulnerabilities and trust.

Email Spoofing

Email spoofing is a prevalent cybercriminals tactic used to create deceptive emails that appear to originate from a legitimate source. By manipulating the email header information, attackers can forge the "From" address to mimic that of a trusted entity, such as a colleague, supervisor, or a well-known business contact. This tactic tricks recipients into believing the email is genuine, making them more likely to interact with the content without suspicion.[25]

For example, cybercriminals may craft phishing emails that appear to be from the dealership's IT department, requesting users to update their login credentials or click on a link to access critical information. Unsuspecting employees may comply with these requests, inadvertently revealing sensitive data or falling victim to malware.

Fake Web Sites

Phishing attacks often involve the creation of fake web sites that imitate the appearance of legitimate dealership portals, login pages, or customer service platforms. These web sites are designed to trick users into believing they

---

[25] https://www.csoonline.com/article/514515/what-is-phishing-examples-types-and-techniques.html.

are accessing a genuine site, prompting them to input sensitive information, such as login credentials or financial details.[26]

For instance, attackers may send phishing emails with links to fake login pages, claiming that users must verify their accounts for security purposes. When users click on these links and enter their credentials, the information is captured by cybercriminals, enabling unauthorized access to dealership systems.

Impersonation

Impersonation is a social engineering technique where cybercriminals pretend to be someone the target knows or trusts. This tactic is particularly effective in spear phishing attacks, where attackers research to gather information about specific individuals within the dealership.

Cybercriminals may impersonate trusted colleagues, business partners, or customers using gathered information from social media profiles or publicly available data. They then send personalized phishing emails, making their messages more convincing and likely to be acted upon by the target.

Urgency and Emotional Manipulation

Phishing emails often use urgency and emotional manipulation to create a sense of pressure and urgency for the recipient to take immediate action. Attackers may claim that the recipient's account has been compromised or risk losing access to critical services unless they promptly click on a provided link or provide sensitive information.

By leveraging emotions, such as fear, concern, or excitement, cybercriminals aim to override the recipient's logical thinking, making them more susceptible to falling for the phishing attempt.

Pretexting

Pretexting is a technique where attackers create a fabricated scenario to deceive the target and extract sensitive information. In a phishing context, cybercriminals may pretend to be someone in authority, such as a senior

---

[26] https://www.csoonline.com/article/514515/what-is-phishing-examples-types-and-techniques.html.

manager or IT support personnel, to request confidential data from employees.

For instance, attackers may send phishing emails claiming to be the dealership's CEO, asking employees to share financial information urgently for a confidential project. Unaware of the deception, employees may willingly provide the requested data, falling victim to the attack.

Real-Life Examples of Phishing Attacks on Car Dealerships

Toyota, 2019

In 2019, Toyota Boshoku Corporation, an auto parts supplier for Toyota, fell victim to a sophisticated phishing attack involving social engineering and business email compromise (BEC). The attackers used persuasive techniques to trick a finance executive into changing the recipient's bank account information during a wire transfer. As a result, the company lost a staggering USD 37 million. This incident demonstrates the potential financial impact and devastating consequences of falling victim to a phishing attack. It highlights the need for robust cybersecurity awareness training for employees, especially those handling sensitive financial transactions, to prevent such social engineering exploits.[27]

Lessons learned: Car dealerships must prioritize cybersecurity training to educate employees about the dangers of social engineering and BEC attacks. Implementing strict verification processes for financial transactions can act as additional protection against such phishing attempts.

Info-Stealer Campaign Targets German Car Dealerships and Manufacturers.

In this case, a sophisticated and monthslong phishing campaign targeted German organizations, primarily in the auto-industry sector. The attackers initiated the campaign with seemingly benign emails related to vehicle purchases. These emails were designed to lure employees into opening malicious attachments or clicking on malicious links.

Once the attackers accessed the dealership's systems, they deployed various info-stealing malware. The threat actors registered multiple lookalike domains to deceive their targets further, mimicking existing

---

[27] https://gatefy.com/blog/real-and-famous-cases-social-engineering-attacks/.

German auto businesses. They used these domains to send phishing emails and host their malware infrastructure.

This incident highlights the potential danger of targeted phishing attacks that aim to steal sensitive information from car dealerships and manufacturers. The use of convincing email content and domain impersonation makes it challenging for employees to identify such phishing attempts.[28]

Lessons Learned: Car dealerships should regularly educate their staff about the evolving nature of phishing attacks and the use of social engineering tactics. Implementing robust email security solutions, including advanced threat detection and filtering, can help prevent such phishing emails from reaching employees' inboxes. Regular cybersecurity assessments, such as simulated phishing exercises, can enhance employees' awareness and response to potential threats.

---

[28] https://blog.checkpoint.com/security/a-german-car-attack-on-german-vehicle-businesses/.

CHAPTER 3

RANSOMWARE ATTACKS: EMERGING CYBERSECURITY THREATS TO CAR DEALERSHIPS

A. OVERVIEW OF RANSOMWARE ATTACKS AND THEIR IMPACT ON DEALERSHIPS

In recent years, ransomware attacks have emerged as one of the most menacing and sophisticated cybersecurity threats facing car dealerships. These malicious attacks target dealership systems and operations, seeking to encrypt critical data and hold it hostage until a ransom is paid. Cybercriminals behind ransomware attacks utilize deceptive tactics, such as phishing emails, malicious downloads, or compromised web sites, to gain unauthorized access to dealership networks.

How Ransomware Works

Ransomware infiltrates a dealership's computer network and rapidly spreads across multiple devices, encrypting data. This encryption makes the data inaccessible to dealership employees, paralyzing daily operations. Once the ransomware has taken hold, a ransom demand is presented to the dealership, usually in the form of cryptocurrencies like Bitcoin, as it allows for anonymous transactions.

Impact on Dealership Operations

The impact of a successful ransomware attack on a car dealership can be devastating. Critical business functions are severely disrupted, including customer data management, financial transactions, inventory management, and communication systems. The resulting downtime leads to significant financial losses, missed sales opportunities, and reputational damage.

Financial Implications of Ransom Demands

The ransom demands in ransomware attacks can vary widely, often determined by factors like the size and perceived vulnerability of the dealership. In recent years, ransom demands have escalated, with cybercriminals realizing the potential for significant financial gains by targeting high-value businesses like car dealerships.[29]

---

[29] https://arcticwolf.com/resources/blog/why-auto-dealers-are-prime-targets-for-ransomware-attacks/.

Ways Dealerships Are Vulnerable to Ransomware

Auto Dealerships Store Consumers' Private Data

One of the primary reasons auto dealerships are highly vulnerable to ransomware attacks is the vast amount of valuable data they store. Dealerships routinely collect and retain sensitive information, including customers' personal identifying information (PII) and financial details. This treasure trove of data, such as names, addresses, social security numbers, and banking information, is highly sought after by cybercriminals on the dark web, fetching substantial sums of money. Consequently, ransomware attackers target auto dealerships to exploit this lucrative source of personal data.

By infiltrating dealership networks and encrypting this sensitive data, cybercriminals can effectively hold customer PII hostage, demanding exorbitant ransoms in return for the decryption keys. The potential exposure of customers' private information puts the dealership's reputation and compliance with data protection regulations at serious risk.

Dealerships Haven't Invested in Cybersecurity

A concerning vulnerability in the automotive industry, including auto dealerships, is the need for sufficient investment in cybersecurity. According to a report by CDK Global, only 24 percent of organizations surveyed stated that they increased their cybersecurity spending in the last year. This lack of proactive investment in cybersecurity makes dealerships susceptible to evolving and sophisticated ransomware attacks.

Despite 85 percent of dealerships acknowledging that cybersecurity threats are "very or extremely" important, many organizations remain complacent, underestimating the severity of potential ransomware incidents. Inaction in bolstering cybersecurity defenses is a grave oversight, considering the growing threats cybercriminals pose and the devastating impact of successful ransomware attacks.

Lack of Security Awareness

Did you know less than a third of dealership employees receive security awareness training?[30]

---

[30] https://www.scmagazine.com/news/security-awareness/a-third-of-companies-dont-offer-cybersecurity-training-to-remote-workers.

Phishing attacks continue to be one of the most successful vectors for ransomware deployment, and cybercriminals are adept at leveraging social engineering tactics to exploit human vulnerabilities. Surprisingly, less than a third of dealership employees receive security awareness training, leaving the workforce ill-equipped to detect and thwart phishing attempts effectively.

In the vast world of cyberattacks, approximately 98 percent involve social engineering on some level, emphasizing the critical role of employees as the first line of defense against cyber threats. Dealerships must prioritize frequent and effective security awareness training to educate their employees on identifying and reporting suspicious activities. Failure to provide proactive education leaves dealership staff susceptible to falling victim to phishing emails, which can inadvertently trigger a ransomware attack.

Attackers Understand Reputation Risk and How to Use It to Their Advantage

The success of ransomware attacks is often fueled by cybercriminals' understanding of the reputation risk associated with data breaches. In the case of auto dealerships, where customer trust is paramount, a data breach can have severe consequences on brand reputation and customer loyalty. According to CDK Global, 84 percent of consumers said they would not return to a dealership if their data had been stolen.

This reputational cost is particularly concerning for dealerships as customer loyalty is the bedrock of their business. Ransomware attackers exploit this vulnerability, knowing that organizations would rather pay the ransom than deal with the repercussions of data theft or a complete system meltdown. Succumbing to ransom demands might seem like a quick fix, but it could further erode customer trust, resulting in long-term damage to the dealership's reputation and bottom line.

In light of the significant vulnerabilities auto dealerships face, adopting a proactive approach to cybersecurity is imperative. The next sections of this chapter will delve deeper into the specific tactics employed by cybercriminals in ransomware attacks. We will explore real-life examples of ransomware incidents that have targeted car dealerships, examining the consequences and lessons learned from these incidents. Additionally, we will discuss best practices for ransomware prevention and incident response, empowering dealerships to build a strong defense against this evolving and dangerous cybersecurity threat.[31]

B. RECENT CASES OF RANSOMWARE ATTACKS TARGETING AUTOMOTIVE ORGANIZATIONS

Ransomware attacks have become a significant cybersecurity threat for automotive organizations, including car dealerships. These attacks have disrupted operations, compromised sensitive data, and caused financial losses. Examining recent case studies of ransomware attacks targeting automotive dealerships sheds light on the tactics employed by attackers and underscores the importance of robust cybersecurity measures and incident response plans.

Kia Motors America (KMA): Suspected DoppelPaymer Ransomware Attack

Automaker Kia Motors America (KMA) faced a suspected DoppelPaymer ransomware attack that affected internal and customer-facing systems. The ransomware gang claimed responsibility for the attack and demanded a staggering $20 million worth of Bitcoin to decrypt files and prevent sensitive data from being leaked online.

However, KMA denied being subject to a ransomware attack but acknowledged an extended system outage affecting services, such as Mobile UVO link apps, payment services, phone services, owner portal, and dealerships' internal systems. Buyers could not pick up their cars due to the system outage caused by the suspected ransomware attack.

Bleeping Computer obtained a ransomware note from the DoppelPaymer threat actors claiming to have attacked KIA's parent company, Hyundai Motor America. The attackers threatened to publish the exfiltrated data if KMA failed to negotiate a settlement within two to three weeks. They also threatened to increase the ransom from 404 Bitcoins (worth about $20 million) to 600 Bitcoins (about $30 million).

This incident underscores the severity of ransomware attacks and the potential consequences for automotive organizations. It highlights the

---

[31] https://www.autoremarketing.com/ar/84-percent-buyers-would-shun-their-dealership-after-data-breach/.

critical need for robust cybersecurity defenses and incident response plans to mitigate the impact of such attacks.[32]

Lessons Learned and the Importance of Robust Cybersecurity Measures

The recent ransomware attacks targeting automotive organizations offer critical lessons and underscore the necessity of robust cybersecurity measures.

Invest in Cybersecurity Practices

Automotive organizations, including car dealerships, must invest significantly in cybersecurity. Proactive spending on cybersecurity defenses is far more cost-effective than dealing with the aftermath of a ransomware attack, which can result in financial losses, reputational damage, and customer attrition.

Employee Security Awareness Training

Secondly, employee security awareness training is crucial in combatting ransomware attacks, particularly those initiated through social engineering tactics like phishing. Educating employees to recognize and report suspicious activities can prevent accidental clicks on malicious links and attachments, thwarting ransomware attempts.

Testing and Improving Incident Response Plans

Automotive dealerships should develop and regularly test their incident response plans. A well-prepared response can mitigate the impact of an attack, limit the spread of ransomware, and expedite recovery.

Working with Cybersecurity Experts

Lastly, enhancing partnerships with cybersecurity experts and law enforcement agencies can facilitate timely threat intelligence sharing and incident response coordination. Automobile dealerships can proactively strengthen their cybersecurity posture by staying informed about the latest ransomware threats.

---

[32] https://www.cpomagazine.com/cyber-security/kia-motors-america-suffers-a-20-million-suspected-doppelpaymer-ransomware-attack/.

C. MITIGATION STRATEGIES AND BEST PRACTICES TO PREVENT AND RESPOND TO RANSOMWARE INCIDENTS IN CAR DEALERSHIPS

Ransomware attacks pose a significant threat to car dealerships, with potentially devastating consequences for their operations, reputation, and customer trust. Implementing robust cybersecurity measures and adopting best practices can help prevent ransomware incidents and effectively respond to potential attacks. Here are essential mitigation strategies and best practices that car dealerships should consider:

Regular Data Backups

Regularly backing up critical data is one of the most effective strategies to safeguard against ransomware attacks. Car dealerships should implement a comprehensive backup plan that includes regular and automated backups of essential systems, databases, customer data, and other critical information. These backups should be stored securely in isolated and offline locations to prevent them from being compromised during attacks. In a ransomware incident, having recent and reliable backups can help restore operations without paying the ransom.

Endpoint Security Solutions

Endpoints, such as employee workstations and mobile devices, are often the entry points for ransomware attacks. Deploying robust endpoint security solutions, including advanced antivirus software, intrusion detection systems, and behavior-based analytics, can help detect and block ransomware before it spreads across the network. Endpoint security solutions should be kept up to date and configured to apply security patches and updates to mitigate vulnerabilities automatically.

Network Segmentation

Network segmentation is a critical practice that involves dividing the dealership's computer network into smaller, isolated segments. By restricting lateral movement within the computer network, even if one component is compromised by ransomware, the attacker's ability to infect other parts of the network is limited. Segmented networks also enable better control and monitoring of network traffic, enhancing the ability to detect and respond to abnormal activities.

Employee Training and Awareness

Educating employees about the risks of ransomware and social engineering tactics is crucial in preventing successful attacks. Regular security awareness training should cover identifying phishing emails, suspicious attachments, and deceptive web sites. Employees should be encouraged to promptly report suspicious activities to the IT team or compliance officer. Additionally, simulated phishing exercises can help assess training effectiveness and identify improvement areas.

Multifactor Authentication

Implementing multifactor authentication adds an extra layer of security to user accounts, making it more challenging for attackers to gain unauthorized access. MFA requires users to provide additional verification, such as a one-time code sent to their mobile device and password. Enforcing MFA for critical systems and privileged accounts can significantly reduce the risk of unauthorized access and ransomware infection.

Regular Security Assessments and Penetration Testing

Regular security assessments and penetration testing can help identify potential vulnerabilities and weaknesses in the dealership's cybersecurity defenses. Regular testing allows for proactive remediation of security gaps and helps ensure that security measures remain effective against evolving ransomware threats.

CHAPTER 4

DATA BREACHES: SAFEGUARDING CUSTOMER INFORMATION IN CAR DEALERSHIPS

A. IMPORTANCE OF PROTECTING CUSTOMER DATA IN CAR DEALERSHIPS

In today's technologically driven world, the criticality of safeguarding customer information must be balanced for car dealerships in the US. As customers engage with dealerships, they provide sensitive personal information, creating a gold mine of data that must be protected at all costs. Research suggests that protecting customer data should always be a top priority for dealerships—as it maintains compliance with various rules and regulations, safeguards their reputation, and avoids potential financial losses. Prioritizing data security requires a comprehensive approach that extends to every level of the organization.[33] This section highlights the importance of ensuring robust data protection measures in car dealerships. It delves into the value of customer data, privacy concerns, legal obligations, and the potential consequences of data breaches.

The Value of Customer Data

Customer data has evolved into a valuable strategic asset for car dealerships. The information collected during interactions, such as test drives, financial transactions, and service appointments, offers insights into customer preferences, behaviors, and buying habits. By harnessing this data effectively, dealerships can personalize their marketing efforts, tailor promotions, and provide exceptional customer experiences.[34] Understanding customers' needs and preferences not only improves sales and customer retention but also enhances the overall reputation of the dealership.

Privacy Concerns and Legal Obligations

As car dealerships amass extensive personal information, customers trust these establishments to keep their data secure and confidential. This trust comes with great responsibility. The US has a complex web of data privacy regulations at the federal and state levels. These laws, such as the California Consumer Privacy Act and the Gramm-Leach-Bliley Act, mandate how customer data should be collected, stored, and used. Failure to comply

---

[33] https://www.cbtnews.com/shifting-focus-making-your-dealerships-data-work-for-you/.
[34] https://www.mckinsey.com/capabilities/risk-and-resilience/our-insights/the-consumer-data-opportunity-and-the-privacy-imperative.

with these regulations can result in severe penalties, regulatory fines, and reputational damage.[35]

Potential Reputational Damage and Legal Consequences

Data breaches can have far-reaching consequences for car dealerships. When sensitive customer data falls into the wrong hands due to a breach, it exposes customers to identity theft, financial fraud, and other malicious activities. The fallout from such incidents can severely damage the dealership's reputation, erode customer trust, and lead to customer churn. Negative publicity surrounding a data breach can deter potential customers from engaging with the dealership, impacting its revenue and market position. Further, legal consequences, including class action lawsuits and regulatory actions, may result in substantial financial losses.

Ensuring Data Protection: Best Practices

To mitigate the risks associated with data breaches, car dealerships must adopt a proactive approach to data protection. Here are some best practices to safeguard customer information:

a. Implement robust security measures. Dealerships should invest in state-of-the-art cybersecurity solutions, including firewalls, intrusion detection systems, and encryption protocols, to protect data from unauthorized access.

b. Conduct regular security audits. Regular assessments of the dealership's security infrastructure can identify and address potential vulnerabilities before cybercriminals exploit them.

c. Educate employees on data protection. Training employees on best practices and cybersecurity awareness can create a strong human firewall against social engineering attacks like phishing and prevent accidental data breaches.

d. Adopt secure data storage and transmission practices. Dealerships should use secure databases and encrypted communication channels to store and transmit customer data, reducing the risk of interception during data transfer. The International Federation of

---

[35] https://www2.deloitte.com/us/en/insights/topics/risk-management/consumer-data-privacy-strategies.html.

Red Cross and Red Crescent Societies (IFRC) provides a set of principles and practices to ensure that personal data is collected, used, and protected in a way that considers individuals' privacy and any risks that may come to them from not adequately safeguarding their data.[36], [37]

e. Develop an incident response plan. Preparing an effective incident response plan ensures that the dealership can respond swiftly and effectively during a data breach, minimizing the damage and facilitating a faster recovery.

B. COMMON CAUSES AND CONSEQUENCES OF DATA BREACHES IN THE AUTOMOTIVE INDUSTRY

Data breaches in the automotive industry have become a growing concern, posing significant risks to car dealerships and other automotive organizations. Despite advancements in cybersecurity, data breaches continue to occur due to various factors. This section explores the common causes of data breaches in the automotive industry, shedding light on human error, weak security controls, and insider threats. Additionally, it delves into the potential consequences of these breaches, including financial loss, regulatory penalties, erosion of customer trust, and legal liabilities.

Human Error

Human error is one of the leading causes of data breaches in the automotive industry. Dealership employees who handle sensitive customer information daily may inadvertently make mistakes that compromise data security. These errors could include sending sensitive information to the wrong recipient, falling victim to phishing attacks, or failing to follow proper data handling protocols.

For instance, an employee might mistakenly attach a customer's financial documents to the wrong email and inadvertently share them with unauthorized parties. Such lapses in judgment can have severe consequences, leading to data breaches and putting the dealership at risk of legal and financial repercussions.

---

[36] https://preparecenter.org/sites/default/files/handout3dataprotectionfaqs210618.pdf.
[37] https://www.ifrc.org/document/data-protection-overview-and-best-practices.

Weak Security Controls

Another significant factor contributing to data breaches is the presence of weak security controls within automotive organizations. Outdated or improperly configured security systems can leave vulnerabilities that cybercriminals exploit to gain unauthorized access to sensitive data.

For example, inadequate encryption practices might expose customer data to unauthorized access during transmission. At the same time, weak password policies may enable attackers to guess or brute force their way into dealership systems. Additionally, promptly applying security updates and patches can leave software and systems vulnerable to known exploits.

Insider Threats

Insider threats pose a unique challenge to data security within the automotive industry. Employees with authorized access to sensitive data may intentionally or inadvertently misuse their privileges to gain unauthorized access or disclose confidential information.

Insiders can be disgruntled employees seeking revenge, individuals coerced by external threat actors or even employees inadvertently disclosing sensitive data due to insufficient training. Detecting and mitigating insider threats requires continuous monitoring, access controls, and comprehensive security awareness programs.

Consequences of Data Breaches in the Automotive Industry

Data breaches in the automotive industry can have severe consequences, impacting the dealership's financial health, reputation, and regulatory compliance. The following are some of the significant consequences that automotive organizations may face:

Financial Loss

Data breaches can lead to significant financial losses for car dealerships. Addressing the aftermath of a breach requires extensive investigation, remediation efforts, and potential legal fees. Additionally, data breaches can result in lawsuits from affected customers seeking compensation for damages caused by exposing their personal information.

Regulatory Penalties

Car dealerships are subject to various data protection laws and regulations, including the California Consumer Privacy Act and the Gramm-Leach-Bliley Act Noncompliance with these regulations can result in hefty fines and penalties imposed by regulatory authorities.

For example, a dealership with inadequate data security measures may face fines from the Federal Trade Commission (FTC) for violating consumer privacy laws. These fines can amount to millions of dollars, posing a significant financial burden to the organization.

Erosion of Customer Trust

The most damaging consequence of a data breach is the erosion of customer trust. When a dealership fails to protect customer data, it sends a message of negligence and disregard for customer privacy. This loss of trust can lead to declining customer loyalty and business as customers seek more reliable and secure alternatives.

Customers are increasingly sensitive to data privacy issues, and a single data breach can lead to a significant loss of customers who may take their business elsewhere, impacting the dealership's revenue and market share.

Reputational Damage

Data breaches generate negative publicity and media attention, tarnishing the dealership's reputation. News of a breach can spread rapidly through social media and news outlets, causing long-term damage to the organization's image.

A dealership's reputation is crucial for attracting new customers and retaining existing ones. A data breach can create a lasting perception of the dealership as untrustworthy or negligent, affecting its ability to compete in the market and hindering business growth.

Legal Liabilities

Data breaches may also expose car dealerships to legal liabilities. In addition to regulatory fines, affected customers may file lawsuits against the dealership for failing to protect their personal information adequately.

These lawsuits can result in costly settlements and legal fees, further adding to the financial impact of the data breach. Furthermore, legal actions can prolong the recovery process and extend the negative impact on the dealership's reputation.

C. STRATEGIES FOR SECURING CUSTOMER INFORMATION AND COMPLYING WITH DATA PRIVACY REGULATIONS

Protecting customer information is of utmost importance for car dealerships. In today's digitally connected world, sensitive data is constantly at risk from cyber threats. Implementing robust data security measures and complying with data privacy regulations is crucial to safeguarding customer information and maintaining trust. This section presents practical strategies for securing customer information and ensuring compliance with data privacy regulations, focusing on strong access controls, encryption, data classification, incident response plans, and adherence to the California Consumer Privacy Act and other states' automotive data privacy regulations.

Strong Access Controls

Implementing strong access controls is the foundation of data security. Car dealerships should adopt the principle of least privilege, ensuring that employees only have access to the data necessary for their job functions. It reduces the risk of unauthorized data access and minimizes potential damage in case of a breach.

Two-factor authentication (2FA) should be enforced for all accounts accessing sensitive information. 2FA adds an extra layer of protection, requiring users to provide an additional form of identification beyond passwords, such as a one-time code sent to their mobile devices. 2FA requires users to provide two different authentication factors (usually something they know and something they have), adding an extra layer of security. On the other hand, multifactor authentication goes further by incorporating more than two authentication factors, which can include something the user is (biometrics) for enhanced protection against unauthorized access.

Regular access rights reviews and audits should also be conducted to identify and revoke unnecessary privileges, ensuring access controls remain up-to-date and effective.

Encryption

Encryption is a fundamental safeguard against data breaches. Car dealerships should implement end-to-end encryption for data in transit and at rest. Encrypting sensitive information ensures that even if data is intercepted or stolen, it remains unreadable and unusable to unauthorized parties.

Encryption should be applied to all communications, including emails, file transfers, and customer data databases. Employing industry-standard encryption algorithms and adhering to best practices for key management is essential to maintain the integrity and confidentiality of customer information.

Data Classification and Segmentation

Correctly classifying data based on its sensitivity level is essential for data protection. Car dealerships should categorize customer information into different tiers, such as public, internal, and confidential data. It enables the organization to apply appropriate security measures based on the data's classification.

Segmentation of networks and data is equally important. By separating sensitive customer data from less critical information, dealerships can limit the impact of a potential breach and make it more challenging for attackers to access high-value data.

Incident Response Plans

A well-defined incident response plan is critical for the timely and effective handling of data breaches. Car dealerships should develop comprehensive incident response plans that outline clear procedures for identifying, containing, and mitigating security incidents.

The plan should designate specific roles and responsibilities for incident response team members and communication protocols to ensure a coordinated response. Regular testing and simulation exercises of the incident response plan can help identify weaknesses and improve efficiency.

Compliance with Data Privacy Regulations

Car dealerships operating in different regions must comply with data privacy regulations specific to those jurisdictions. This includes the General Data

Protection Regulation in the European Union, the California Consumer Privacy Act, and other states' data privacy regulations.

a. General Data Protection Regulation

For dealerships serving customers in the European Union, GDPR compliance is essential. The GDPR enforces strict requirements for the processing and protection of personal data of EU citizens, regardless of where the organization is located.

Dealerships must appoint a data protection officer (DPO) responsible for overseeing data protection efforts and ensuring compliance with the GDPR's principles. Customers must obtain consent before processing their data, and individuals have the right to access, rectify, and erase their data upon request.

b. California Consumer Privacy Act

Car dealerships operating in California or handling the personal information of California residents are subject to the CCPA. The CCPA grants California consumers specific rights regarding confidential data and imposes obligations on businesses to ensure data privacy.

Compliance with the CCPA requires transparency about data collection practices, allowing consumers to opt out of the sale of their personal information and providing a transparent process for consumers to exercise their rights under the CCPA.

Regular Training and Awareness Programs

Car dealerships should invest in regular cybersecurity training and awareness programs for all employees. Training sessions should cover identifying and avoiding phishing emails, recognizing social engineering tactics, and understanding best practices for data security.

Employee awareness plays a crucial role in preventing data breaches caused by human error. When employees are knowledgeable about cybersecurity risks and their responsibilities in protecting customer information, they become a vital line of defense against cyber threats.

CHAPTER 5

SOCIAL ENGINEERING: MANIPULATING THE HUMAN ELEMENT IN DEALERSHIP CYBERSECURITY

A. UNDERSTANDING SOCIAL ENGINEERING TACTICS USED IN CYBERATTACKS

In the ever-evolving landscape of cybersecurity threats, social engineering is a particularly insidious and effective tactic cybercriminals use to exploit human vulnerabilities. Car dealerships, like many other organizations, are prime targets for social engineering attacks due to the wealth of valuable customer data they possess. Understanding attackers' tactics is crucial for dealership employees and management to recognize and defend against these manipulative techniques. This section explores some common social engineering tactics cybercriminals use in the automotive industry, including pretexting, phishing, and baiting, shedding light on the psychological manipulation involved in these attacks.

Pretexting

Pretexting is a social engineering technique in which an attacker creates a fabricated scenario or pretext to trick individuals into divulging sensitive information. The attacker assumes a false identity and poses as trustworthy or authoritative to gain the target's confidence.[38]

In car dealerships, an attacker might pose as a customer, a colleague from another department, or even an IT support technician. By crafting a believable pretext, the attacker aims to manipulate dealership employees into revealing sensitive data or providing unauthorized access to systems.

For instance, an attacker could call the dealership's reception and pretend to be a customer experiencing an urgent issue with their vehicle. The attacker may use this ruse to gather personal information, such as account details, driver's license numbers, or payment information.

Phishing

Phishing is one of the most prevalent social engineering tactics cybercriminals use. In a phishing attack, attackers send deceptive emails, text messages, or instant messages, impersonating legitimate entities or trusted sources to lure recipients into revealing sensitive information or clicking on malicious links.[39]

---

[38] https://www.ibm.com/topics/pretexting.
[39] https://socradar.io/automotive-industry-under-ransomware-attacks/.

In the automotive industry, phishing emails appear as official communications from car manufacturers, banks, or dealership management. These emails often contain urgent messages, such as warranty expiration notices or safety recalls, to create a sense of urgency and prompt the recipient to take immediate action.

Clicking on links within phishing emails can lead to the installation of malware, enabling attackers to gain unauthorized access to the dealership's network or compromise customer data.

Baiting

Baiting is a social engineering technique that exploits human curiosity and greed. Attackers entice targets with the promise of something desirable, such as free software, discounts, or exclusive offers, to trick them into downloading malicious files or revealing sensitive information.[40]

In the automotive dealership, baiting tactics may involve offering "exclusive" vehicle deals or promotions that require recipients to provide personal information to claim the offer. Additionally, attackers might leave infected USB drives or other devices in public spaces, hoping employees will plug them into dealership computers, unwittingly installing malware.

The Psychological Manipulation

At the core of social engineering tactics lies psychological manipulation. Attackers leverage emotional triggers like fear, urgency, curiosity, and greed to bypass rational thinking and invoke an immediate response from their targets.

- Fear. Attackers may create fear by threatening severe consequences, such as legal action or financial losses, if the target does not comply with their demands.
- Urgency. By instilling a sense of urgency, attackers push targets to act quickly without considering the consequences, making them more likely to divulge sensitive information or click on malicious links.

---

[40] https://learn.saylor.org/mod/book/view.php?id=29612&chapterid=5160.

- Curiosity. The promise of "exclusive" or "confidential" information piques curiosity, enticing targets to explore further, often without verifying the source or legitimacy of the request.
- Greed. Exploiting the desire for financial gain or personal benefit, attackers entice targets with offers that seem too good to pass up, leading them to take actions that compromise security.

Raising Awareness and Building Resilience

Mitigating social engineering threats requires a multifaceted approach that combines technology, policies, and user awareness. Car dealerships must prioritize cybersecurity training and education to empower employees with the knowledge and skills to recognize and resist social engineering attacks.

Regular and engaging training sessions can simulate real-world scenarios and equip employees with practical strategies to verify the legitimacy of requests and emails. Employees should be encouraged to report suspicious activities promptly, creating a culture of cybersecurity vigilance within the organization.[41], [42]

Furthermore, car dealerships should implement robust email filtering and anti-phishing technologies to detect and block malicious emails before they reach employees' inboxes. Robust access controls and network segmentation can limit the impact of successful social engineering attacks, reducing the risk of unauthorized access to critical systems and data.

Conclusion

Social engineering attacks pose a significant threat to car dealerships, leveraging human vulnerabilities to gain unauthorized access to sensitive information and compromise cybersecurity defenses. Understanding attackers' tactics, such as pretexting, phishing, and baiting, is essential for building resilience and fostering a cybersecurity-aware culture within dealerships.

---

[41] https://ieeexplore.ieee.org/document/8615162.
[42] https://ieeexplore.ieee.org/abstract/document/8854548.

B. METHODS EMPLOYED BY CYBERCRIMINALS TO EXPLOIT DEALERSHIP EMPLOYEES

In the ongoing battle against cyber threats, social engineering is one of the most potent weapons in a cybercriminal's arsenal. Cybercriminals use manipulative methods to exploit dealership employees and gain unauthorized access to sensitive information. This section delves into some common social engineering tactics cybercriminals employ to manipulate dealership employees, including impersonation, elicitation, and the exploitation of trust. Real-life examples will be provided to illustrate how these methods are used to compromise cybersecurity defenses and extract valuable data.

Impersonation

Impersonation is a social engineering technique where cybercriminals masquerade as someone else to gain trust and manipulate their targets. In the context of car dealerships, attackers might impersonate customers, colleagues, or even senior management to deceive employees into divulging sensitive information or granting unauthorized access to systems.

Elicitation

Elicitation is a tactic used by cybercriminals to extract information from employees without arousing suspicion. Attackers engage in casual conversations with dealership employees, skillfully steering the discussion toward sensitive topics and extracting valuable data.

Exploitation of Trust

Cybercriminals often exploit the trust between colleagues and employees to execute social engineering attacks. By leveraging existing relationships, attackers can manipulate employees into sharing sensitive data or clicking on malicious links.

Baiting

Baiting is a social engineering tactic that preys on human curiosity and desire for gain. Attackers offer enticing bait, such as free software, discounts, or exclusive content, to trick employees into downloading malicious files or revealing sensitive information.[43]

Real-Life Example

According to a report from WardsAuto, let's take a hypothetical assumption to create a real-life example.[44]

A car dealership employee inadvertently caused a major security breach when they lost their company-issued laptop during a business trip. The laptop contained sensitive customer information, including personal data and financial details. Despite the dealership's security protocols, the employee failed to encrypt the laptop's hard drive or use additional security measures, making it susceptible to unauthorized access.

In a stroke of bad luck, the lost laptop was found by a cybercriminal who recognized the potential treasure trove of information it contained. Using the data from the laptop, the attacker gained access to the dealership's network and monitored every click and keystroke made by employees, allowing them to gather valuable information about the dealership's operations and customer interactions.

The cybercriminal crafted a cunning social engineering scheme to exploit the situation further. As a colleague from another dealership branch, the attacker contacted other employees via email and phone calls, requesting sensitive security and financial information under the guise of an urgent business matter. Unaware of the ongoing data breach and trusting the familiar name, several employees fell victim to the deception and disclosed confidential information to the cybercriminal.

In addition, another unsuspecting employee unknowingly plugged in a seemingly harmless flash drive found lying around the dealership. Unknown to them, the flash drive was infected with malware, allowing the attacker to gain a foothold in the dealership's network, further expanding their access and control.

The situation escalated rapidly as the cybercriminal exploited these human errors and used the gathered information to execute more targeted and sophisticated attacks. The consequences were severe, ranging from

---

[43] https://www.exabeam.com/information-security/top-8-social-engineering-techniques-and-how-to-prevent-them-2022/.

[44] https://www.wardsauto.com/sites/wardsauto.com/files/uploads/2016/TheBigStory-Dealer-1016-2.pdf.

financial losses due to unauthorized transactions to compromising customer data, leading to a loss of client trust and potentially damaging the dealership's reputation.

Mitigation Strategies

To defend against social engineering attacks, car dealerships must implement robust cybersecurity measures and educate their employees about the tactics used by cybercriminals. Here are some strategies to mitigate the risk of falling victim to social engineering:

- Comprehensive training. Regular cybersecurity training sessions should be conducted for all dealership employees, focusing on recognizing and responding to social engineering tactics. Employees should be encouraged to question unusual requests, verify information with trusted sources, and report suspicious activities promptly.[45]
- Strong access controls. Implement strict access controls to limit employee access to sensitive data and critical systems. Only authorized personnel should have privileged access, and multifactor authentication should be used to add an extra layer of security.
- Email filtering and phishing tests. Deploy advanced email filtering and anti-phishing technologies to detect and block malicious emails before they reach employees' inboxes. Regular phishing simulation tests can help assess employees' susceptibility to phishing attacks and tailor training accordingly.
- Incident response plan. Develop a comprehensive incident response plan that outlines the steps to be taken in case of a social engineering attack. This plan should include procedures for reporting incidents, isolating affected systems, and conducting thorough investigations.
- Security awareness culture. Foster a culture of cybersecurity awareness within the dealership by promoting vigilance and responsible information handling among employees. Reward and recognize employees who demonstrate exemplary cybersecurity practices.

---

[45] https://www.forbes.com/sites/forbestechcouncil/2022/07/22/social-engineering-threats-and-mitigation/.

- Monitoring and detection. Implement robust monitoring and detection systems to identify suspicious activities and potential social engineering attempts. Behavioral analytics and anomaly detection can help detect unusual access or data usage patterns.
- Data encryption and classification. Encrypt sensitive data in transit and at rest to protect it from unauthorized access. Implement data classification policies to ensure sensitive information is appropriately handled and restricted.
- Regular data backups. Conduct regular data backups to ensure that critical information is securely stored and can be recovered in case of a ransomware attack or data breach.
- Compliance with data privacy regulations. Stay up-to-date with data privacy regulations, such as the General Data Protection Regulation and the California Consumer Privacy Act and ensure that the dealership's data handling practices comply. It includes obtaining customer consent for data processing, providing access and deletion rights, and implementing data retention policies.
- Vendor and third-party risk management. If the dealership works with third-party vendors or service providers, ensure they have robust cybersecurity practices. Conduct regular security assessments and due diligence on vendors to minimize the risk of social engineering attacks through third-party channels.
- Continuous improvement. Cybersecurity is an ongoing process. Continuously assess and improve the dealership's security measures, policies, and practices to stay ahead of evolving social engineering tactics.[46]

C. TRAINING AND AWARENESS PROGRAMS TO COMBAT SOCIAL ENGINEERING THREATS

Social engineering continues to be a potent weapon employed by cybercriminals. Car dealerships must recognize that the human element is their greatest strength and vulnerability in cybersecurity. Comprehensive training and awareness programs are essential to combat social engineering

---

[46] https://link.springer.com/chapter/10.1007/978-3-319-58424-9_35.

threats effectively. These programs empower employees with the knowledge and skills to recognize and respond to social engineering tactics, bolstering the dealership's overall cybersecurity posture.

Importance of Training and Awareness Programs

Security awareness training is a proactive approach to building a cybersecurity-aware culture within the dealership. Car dealerships can foster a vigilant and informed workforce by educating employees about social engineering threats and their potential consequences. These programs serve as a crucial defense against cyber threats, making employees the first and often the last line of protection.

Components of Effective Security Awareness Training

Simulated Phishing Exercises.

Simulated phishing exercises are instrumental in gauging the dealership employees' susceptibility to phishing attacks. By sending mock phishing emails to employees, car dealerships can assess their response rates and identify vulnerable individuals. These exercises provide valuable insights into the areas that require additional training and reinforcement.

Role-Based Training

Different roles within the dealership have distinct cybersecurity responsibilities. Tailoring training content to specific job functions ensures that employees receive relevant information and guidance. For instance, finance personnel may require additional training on financial transaction security, while IT administrators need to be well-versed in system access controls.

Reporting Mechanisms

Establishing clear and accessible reporting mechanisms is crucial for encouraging employees to report suspicious activities promptly. Anonymity and nonpunitive reporting procedures can alleviate fears of repercussions and encourage employees to come forward if they encounter potential security threats.

Phishing Resistance Techniques

Training should teach employees to recognize phishing attempts by identifying red flags, such as unfamiliar senders, suspicious URLs, and urgent requests for sensitive information. They should also be educated about the importance of independently verifying requests from unfamiliar or unexpected sources.

Password Hygiene and Multifactor Authentication

Employees should be educated about the significance of strong password management practices. Encouraging complex and unique passwords and implementing MFA can significantly enhance the dealership's security posture.

Social Engineering Awareness

Training programs should delve into the psychology behind social engineering tactics, helping employees understand the manipulation techniques used by cybercriminals. By raising awareness of the emotional triggers used in social engineering attacks, employees can be better equipped to identify and resist these tactics.

The Role of Employees in Detecting and Reporting Suspicious Activities

Empowering employees to become active participants in cybersecurity defense is crucial. Car dealerships can create a collaborative security culture by emphasizing their role in detecting and reporting suspicious activities. Employees should be encouraged to report any anomalies, potential phishing emails, or unauthorized requests they encounter. Providing clear guidance on how and where to report such incidents without fear of retaliation can help ensure that potential threats are promptly addressed.[47]

Recognizing employees who contribute to maintaining a secure environment can further incentivize proactive behavior. Regular acknowledgment and rewards for individuals who spot and report potential

---

[47] https://www.icaew.com/regulation/regulatory-news/2021-june/the-role-of-the-mlro-beyond-compliance.

threats can reinforce the importance of cybersecurity awareness throughout the dealership.[48]

Conclusion

In the battle against social engineering threats, continuous training and awareness programs are indispensable tools that car dealerships must embrace. These programs equip employees with the knowledge and skills to recognize, resist, and effectively report social engineering tactics. By fostering a cybersecurity-aware culture and involving employees as active defenders, car dealerships can enhance their resilience against social engineering threats, safeguard customer information, and maintain a strong defense posture in the ever-evolving cyber threat landscape.

---

[48] https://www.icaew.com/regulation/regulatory-news/2021-june/the-role-of-the-mlro-beyond-compliance.

CHAPTER 6

REGULATORY COMPLIANCE: NAVIGATING FTC GUIDELINES FOR CAR DEALERSHIPS

A. OVERVIEW OF FTC REGULATIONS APPLICABLE TO CAR DEALERSHIPS

Car dealerships handle vast amounts of customer data and must comply with various regulations to protect consumer interests and maintain data privacy. The Federal Trade Commission is a significant regulatory body that plays a crucial role in overseeing data security practices in the automotive industry. Per FTC, dealerships had to comply with the new rules by December 9, 2022.[49] In this section, we will provide an overview of FTC regulations relevant to car dealerships, focusing on guidelines related to the protection of consumer information, advertising practices, and deceptive trade practices.

Protection of Consumer Information

Under the FTC Safeguards Rule, car dealerships must implement data security measures to safeguard nonpublic personal information (NPI) collected from consumers. NPI includes sensitive information, such as customer names, addresses, Social Security numbers, credit card details, and driver's license numbers.

To ensure compliance, car dealerships should consider making three separate disclosures.

1. General Vehicle Data Collection Disclosure

Car dealerships should inform consumers about the capability of vehicles to collect, store, and share data that may fall under the definition of NPI. This disclosure should direct consumers to the Original Equipment Manufacturer's (OEM) privacy policy while considering disclosing specific categories of sensitive information, such as owner's identity, geolocation, biometrics, and driver behavior information.[50]

2. Data Sharing Disclosure

If the dealership has a data-sharing agreement with the OEM, a disclosure should be made to inform consumers about the data shared between the dealership and the OEM. The specific details of this disclosure should

---

[49] https://www.seyfarth.com/news-insights/ftc-begins-process-to-adopt-rules-for-new-car-dealer-advertising-and-sales.html.

[50] https://www.ftc.gov/business-guidance/industry/automobiles.

be reviewed with legal counsel due to variations in OEM agreements and state laws on data protection.

3. Vehicle Data Stored Locally Disclosure

Dealerships should disclose the reasonable technical, administrative, and physical safeguards they have in place to protect the NPI stored locally in vehicles. The only effective safeguard for this data is to delete it after each customer's vehicle use or upon customer request.

Vehicle Data Deletion

Car dealerships need a documented process and record-keeping system for vehicle data deletion to maintain compliance with FTC regulations. Specific instances requiring data deletion include the following:

- Trade-ins and lease returns: Vehicle data deletion should occur when the dealership acquires a trade-in or lease return vehicle before selling it.
- Vehicles purchased at auctions: Unless the auction provides evidence of vehicle data deletion, the dealership should delete the data after possessing the vehicle.
- Repossessed vehicles: If the recovery agent does not provide evidence of data deletion, the dealership should delete the data upon possessing the repossessed vehicle.
- Vehicles destined for wholesale: The dealership should delete vehicle data before shipping the vehicle to the auction or delete it during the listing process for online auctions.
- Test drives, employee vehicle use, and loaners: Vehicle data should be deleted before offering it to another customer during the vehicle return process.
- Service or warranty work: The dealership should specify in servicing or warranty agreements that they do not authorize anyone to access or use vehicle data while the vehicle is in their possession, except as necessary to perform the work. Data deletion should occur only if specifically requested by the customer during service.[51]

---

[51] https://advantagegps.com/wp-content/uploads/2022/09/P4C-White-Paper-FTC-Safeguards-Rule-Update-June-2022-FINAL.pdf.

FTC Safeguards Rule Requirements

Car dealerships must implement various measures to comply with the FTC Safeguards Rule. Some key requirements include the following:

- Designating a "qualified individual": Each dealership must appoint a qualified individual responsible for developing, overseeing, monitoring, and enforcing the information security program.
- Periodic risk assessments: Dealerships should conduct periodic risk assessments to guide the updating and enforcement of their information security program.
- Customer information safeguards: Implement safeguards to control the risks identified in risk assessments for all customer information, considering all information provided by the customer as covered under customer information.
- Infrastructure monitoring and assessments: Conduct continuous monitoring or annual penetration testing and biannual vulnerability assessments for the dealership's infrastructure.
- Employee security policies: Implement policies and procedures to ensure employees properly enact and carry out the information security program.
- Security on third parties: Ensure third parties with access to customer information maintain safeguards consistent with the dealership's information security program.
- Incident response plan: Develop and implement a written incident response plan to address any breaches or exposure of customer information.
- Annual reporting: Report in writing, at least annually, to the dealership's board of directors or equivalent governing body on the status of the information security program and compliance with the Safeguards Rule.

Conclusion

Compliance with FTC regulations is vital for car dealerships to protect consumer data, avoid penalties, and maintain consumer trust. By understanding and adhering to the FTC guidelines concerning the protection of consumer information, advertising practices, and deceptive trade practices, car dealerships can demonstrate their commitment to data privacy and ethical business practices. Implementing robust data protection measures and fostering a culture of compliance will benefit the dealership and enhance customer confidence and loyalty.

B. COMPLIANCE REQUIREMENTS AND OBLIGATIONS FOR PROTECTING CONSUMER INFORMATION

Car dealerships handle a vast amount of sensitive consumer information, making data protection a top priority to ensure the security and privacy of their customers. Compliance with regulatory requirements, especially those outlined by the Federal Trade Commission, is essential to safeguard consumer data and maintain trust in the dealership's operations. This section will detail the specific compliance requirements and obligations for car dealerships in protecting consumer information, focusing on key elements, such as Written Information Security Programs (WISPs), risk assessments, and incident response plans.[52]

Written Information Security Programs

A Written Information Security Program is a comprehensive document that outlines the dealership's strategy for safeguarding customer information.[53] The FTC mandates that car dealerships, like other financial institutions, implement a WISP that addresses the following key components:

- Hiring the right professional: The WISP should designate a qualified individual responsible for developing, implementing, and maintaining the dealership's information security program. This individual plays a pivotal role in overseeing data protection measures.
- Identification of information covered: The WISP should clearly define the types of customer information covered under the program, including nonpublic personal information (NPI) and other sensitive data.
- Risk assessments: The WISP should include periodic risk assessments that identify potential vulnerabilities and threats to

---

[52] https://www.ftc.gov/business-guidance/resources/ftcs-privacy-rule-auto-dealers-faqs.
[53] https://blog.sellyautomotive.com/blog/what-used-car-dealerships-must-do-to-comply-with-new-ftc-requirements-a-blog-about-what-ftc-compliance-means-for-automotive-dealers.

consumer information. Risk assessments help prioritize security measures and focus resources on areas of highest risk.

- Administrative, technical, and physical safeguards: The WISP should detail administrative, technical, and physical safeguards to protect customer data. Administrative safeguards include establishing security policies, training employees, and conducting regular audits. Technical safeguards involve implementing encryption, access controls, and intrusion detection systems. Physical safeguards include securing physical access to data storage areas.
- Vendor management: Car dealerships often work with third-party vendors who may have access to consumer information. The WISP should outline guidelines for vendor management and require vendors to maintain adequate security measures.[54]
- Incident response plan: The WISP must include a comprehensive incident response plan that outlines steps to take in case of a data breach or security incident. This plan should facilitate a timely and effective response to mitigate potential consumer harm.

Risk Assessments

Regular risk assessments are critical in identifying and evaluating potential threats to customer information. Car dealerships must conduct these assessments periodically and in response to significant changes in their business operations or information systems.[55] A robust risk assessment process should include the following:

- Identifying information assets: Identify all information assets that contain customer data, such as databases, applications, physical documents, and employee devices.
- Analyzing threats and vulnerabilities: Evaluate potential threats and vulnerabilities to customer data, both internal and external, including human errors, cyberattacks, and natural disasters.
- Assessing impact and likelihood: Determine the potential impact and likelihood of various threats materializing, considering factors like the sensitivity of the data and the effectiveness of existing safeguards.

---

[54] https://www.ftc.gov/business-guidance/resources/ftc-safeguards-rule-what-your-business-needs-know.

[55] https://www.nada.org/index.php/safeguardsrule.

- Prioritizing risk mitigation: Prioritize risk mitigation measures and allocate resources based on the risk assessment findings.
- Updating risk assessments: Regularly update risk assessments to account for changes in the dealership's operations, information systems, and the threat landscape.[56]

Incident Response Plans

Incident response plans are vital to respond promptly and effectively to security incidents or data breaches. The following elements should be included in a dealership's incident response plan:

- Incident identification: Define the process for detecting and identifying security incidents, whether through automated monitoring, employee reports, or third-party alerts.
- Response team and roles: Identify key personnel responsible for responding to incidents, their roles, and the communication channels to report incidents.
- Incident containment and mitigation: Outline steps to contain and mitigate the impact of security incidents to prevent further data exposure.
- Communication protocols: Define procedures for communicating internally and externally during a security incident, including notifying affected individuals, law enforcement, and regulators as required.
- Post-Incident analysis and reporting: Detail post-incident analysis to understand the incident's root cause, lessons learned, and necessary adjustments to prevent future occurrences. Also, report incidents to appropriate authorities as required by regulations.

Employee Training and Awareness

Employees play a crucial role in protecting consumer information. Car dealerships should conduct regular cybersecurity training and awareness programs to educate employees about data protection practices and social

---

[56] https://www.mckinsey.com/~/media/mckinsey/industries/automotive%20and%20 assembly/our%20insights/cybersecurity%20in%20automotive%20mastering%20the%20 challenge/cybersecurity-in-automotive-mastering-the-challenge.pdf.

engineering risks. Training should cover topics, such as identifying phishing attempts, secure password management, and the proper handling of customer information. Encouraging a culture of cybersecurity awareness among employees helps create a vigilant and proactive security posture.

Conclusion

Compliance with FTC guidelines is essential for car dealerships to protect consumer information and maintain their reputation as trustworthy establishments. Implementing a comprehensive Written Information Security Program, conducting periodic risk assessments, and having an effective incident response plan are fundamental steps in safeguarding customer data. By educating employees about data protection best practices and fostering a culture of cybersecurity awareness, car dealerships can effectively protect consumer information and adhere to regulatory requirements. Prioritizing data security will safeguard the dealership's operations and strengthen customer trust and loyalty, ultimately benefiting the entire automotive industry.

C. STEPS TO DEVELOP CYBERSECURITY PLANS IN LINE WITH FTC GUIDELINES

Developing comprehensive cybersecurity plans in line with Federal Trade Commission guidelines is crucial for car dealerships to protect consumer information and comply with data security regulations. These cybersecurity plans should encompass various elements, including risk assessments, privacy impact assessments, ongoing monitoring, and reporting. Car dealerships need to follow specific steps to create robust cybersecurity plans that effectively safeguard customer data and demonstrate compliance with FTC guidelines.[57] Below are the steps needed to develop such cybersecurity plans.

Conduct Privacy Impact Assessments

In addition to risk assessments, car dealerships should conduct Privacy Impact Assessments (PIAs) to assess the impact of collecting, using, and sharing customer data. PIAs help identify potential privacy risks and

---

[57] https://www.ftc.gov/business-guidance/small-businesses/cybersecurity/basics.

ensure data processing practices align with privacy regulations.[58] Key steps in conducting PIAs include the following:

- Identify data collection and use. Map the flow of customer data within the dealership, from collection to storage and sharing. Identify the purpose of data collection and how it will be used.
- Evaluate privacy risks. Assess the privacy risks associated with data processing activities, including the potential impact on individual privacy rights.
- Implement mitigation measures. Develop measures to mitigate identified privacy risks, such as obtaining consent, implementing data access controls, and ensuring data accuracy.
- Ensure compliance with privacy regulations. Review data processing practices to ensure compliance with relevant privacy laws, such as the California Consumer Privacy Act and other states' data privacy regulations.

Establish Policies and Procedures

Develop and document comprehensive policies and procedures to guide employees and stakeholders in implementing cybersecurity measures.[59] These policies and procedures should address the following:

- Data access controls: Establish rules and guidelines for granting access to customer information, ensuring that only authorized personnel can access sensitive data.
- Password management: Implement strong password policies and educate employees on secure password practices, such as using complex passwords and enabling multifactor authentication.
- Incident response plan: Develop an incident response plan that outlines the steps to be taken in case of a data breach or security incident. Clearly define roles and responsibilities for incident response team members.

---

[58] https://www.ftc.gov/business-guidance/resources/ftc-safeguards-rule-what-your-business-needs-know.

[59] https://www.cisecurity.org/-/jssmedia/Project/cisecurity/cisecurity/data/media/files/uploads/2021/11/NIST-Cybersecurity-Framework-Policy-Template-Guide-v2111Online.pdf.

- Vendor M\management: Establish guidelines for evaluating and monitoring third-party vendors with access to customer data, ensuring they maintain adequate security measures.[60]

Implement Ongoing Monitoring and Reporting

Cybersecurity is an ongoing process that requires continuous monitoring and reporting. Car dealerships should establish mechanisms for constant monitoring and timely reporting of security incidents.[61] Key aspects of constant monitoring and reporting include the following:

Continuous monitoring: Implement systems for continuously monitoring information systems, network traffic, and security logs to detect suspicious activities or anomalies.

Incident logging and reporting: Document all security incidents, including attempts and breaches, and report them to appropriate authorities and affected customers, as regulations require.

Periodic security reviews: Conduct regular security reviews and audits to assess cybersecurity measures' effectiveness and identify improvement areas.

Annual reporting: Prepare and submit annual reports on the dealership's information security program and compliance with FTC guidelines to the board of directors or equivalent governing body.

Conclusion

Developing comprehensive cybersecurity plans in line with FTC guidelines is a critical responsibility for car dealerships.[62] Car dealerships can create effective cybersecurity plans that protect consumer information and demonstrate compliance with data security regulations by conducting risk assessments, privacy impact assessments, and documenting policies and procedures. Ongoing monitoring and reporting ensure that cybersecurity measures remain up to date and responsive to emerging threats. Prioritizing cybersecurity measures will safeguard customer data and strengthen customer trust and confidence in the dealership's operations.

---

[60] https://csrc.nist.gov/Projects/Access-Control-Policy-and-Implementation-Guides.

[61] https://www.mckinsey.com/industries/automotive-and-assembly/our-insights/cybersecurity-in-automotive-mastering-the-challenge.

[62] https://www.mckinsey.com/industries/automotive-and-assembly/our-insights/the-race-for-cybersecurity-protecting-the-connected-car-in-the-era-of-new-regulation.

CHAPTER 7

INCIDENT RESPONSE AND RECOVERY STRATEGIES FOR CAR DEALERSHIPS

A. ESTABLISHING AN INCIDENT RESPONSE PLAN TAILORED TO DEALERSHIPS' NEEDS

Establishing a robust incident response plan is of paramount importance for car dealerships. Such a plan is the backbone of an organization's ability to detect, respond to, and recover from cybersecurity incidents and data breaches. By tailoring the incident response plan to the unique requirements of car dealerships, they can ensure a well-coordinated and organized response, thereby minimizing the impact of incidents on customer data and business operations.[63]

This section will guide car dealerships in developing a comprehensive and effective incident response plan encompassing key components, such as incident identification, containment, eradication, and recovery. Additionally, it will address the importance of clear roles, responsibilities, and communication channels to ensure a swift and decisive response to cybersecurity incidents.

Identify Incident Response Team and Key Stakeholders

The first step in establishing an incident response plan is identifying the incident response team and key stakeholders. The incident response team should consist of individuals from different departments, including IT, security, legal, communications, and senior management. Each team member should have clearly defined roles and responsibilities in the event of an incident. The team's composition should reflect the organization's specific needs and expertise, ensuring a diverse skill set to handle various aspects of incident response effectively.[64]

Conduct Risk Assessment and Incident Scenarios

Car dealerships should conduct a comprehensive risk assessment to identify potential cybersecurity threats and vulnerabilities that they might face. Based on this assessment, incident scenarios should be developed, outlining various types of incidents that the dealership might encounter. These

---

[63] https://niada.com/dashboard/changes-to-the-safeguards-rule-and-how-it-applies-to-your-dealership/.

[64] https://www.exabeam.com/incident-response/incident-response-plan/.

scenarios should be carefully analyzed to determine their potential impact on customer data, business operations, and overall reputation.

Develop Incident Response Procedures

The incident response plan should include detailed response procedures for each scenario. These procedures should cover the following stages:

a. Incident identification: Define indicators of compromise and suspicious activities that might indicate a security incident. Implement robust monitoring and detection mechanisms to identify potential incidents promptly. Automated security tools can aid in real-time detection and alerting.

b. Incident containment: Establish clear and effective procedures to prevent the incident from spreading further within the dealership's network and systems. It might involve isolating affected systems, deactivating compromised accounts, or shutting down certain services temporarily.

c. Incident eradication: Determine the incident's root cause and take necessary actions to eliminate the threat from the dealership's systems and networks. Thoroughly investigate the incident to prevent future occurrences.

d. Incident recovery: Develop a well-defined plan for recovering affected systems and data to restore normal business operations as quickly as possible. This may include data restoration from backups and validation of system integrity.[65]

Establish Communication Protocols

Clear and effective communication is essential during incident response. The incident response plan should outline communication protocols for both internal and external stakeholders.[66] Critical aspects of communication protocols include the following:

- Internal communication: Establish channels for communication within the incident response team and other relevant departments.

---

[65] https://www.ibm.com/downloads/cas/JZ38L39E.

[66] https://www.alert-software.com/blog/incident-management-communication.

Define how information should be shared and ensure everyone knows their roles and responsibilities during an incident. Regular meetings and status updates are crucial to maintaining a well-informed team.

- External communication: Determine who should be informed externally during an incident, such as law enforcement, customers, partners, and regulatory authorities. Develop templates for communicating with these stakeholders to ensure consistency and accuracy in the messaging.

Test and Train the Incident Response Plan

Regular testing and training are critical to ensuring the effectiveness of the incident response plan. Car dealerships should conduct tabletop exercises and simulated incident scenarios to evaluate the response team's readiness and identify any gaps in the plan.[67] These exercises can also serve as valuable training opportunities for the team members to understand the procedures better and refine their response skills. Additionally, employees across the organization should receive cybersecurity awareness training to familiarize them with incident response procedures and their respective roles in supporting the response efforts.

Continuously Improve the Incident Response Plan

Incident response plans should be dynamic and subject to continuous improvement. Regularly review and update the plan based on lessons learned from testing and real incidents. Stay informed about emerging cybersecurity threats and adjust response procedures accordingly. Conduct post-incident reviews to identify areas for improvement and implement necessary changes to enhance the plan's effectiveness.

By conducting a comprehensive risk assessment and developing detailed response procedures, dealerships can ensure a proactive and well-coordinated approach to incident detection, containment, eradication, and recovery. Implementing clear communication protocols and regular testing and training exercises will further enhance the team's preparedness to respond to incidents swiftly and decisively. An effective incident response

---

[67] https://www.atlassian.com/incident-management/incident-communication https://www.atlassian.com/incident-management/incident-communication.

plan not only safeguards customer data and business operations but also reinforces the dealership's reputation as a trusted and secure provider of automotive services.

B. EFFECTIVE COMMUNICATION AND COORDINATION DURING CYBER INCIDENTS

In the ever-evolving landscape of cybersecurity threats, car dealerships must prioritize effective communication and coordination during cyber incidents to protect their customers' data, maintain business continuity, and safeguard their reputations. A well-prepared incident response plan is essential, which should include a comprehensive communication strategy and clear coordination protocols.[68] This section explores the critical role of communication and coordination during cyber incidents in car dealerships, delving into the importance of establishing clear internal and external communication channels, collaborating with law enforcement and legal counsel, engaging other relevant stakeholders, and managing public relations.

Establishing Clear Internal Communication Channels

- Incident response team: Car dealerships should form a dedicated incident response team comprising representatives from IT, security, legal, communications, and senior management. This team is the central communication hub during an incident, coordinating all response efforts.
- Communication protocols: The incident response plan should outline clear communication protocols for the incident response team, specifying how team members share information, escalate issues, and coordinate actions. Timely updates are crucial to ensure all stakeholders can make well-informed decisions.
- Regular status updates: Regular status updates should be scheduled to provide all team members with a comprehensive overview of the incident's current status, ongoing response actions, and any strategy changes. These updates maintain situational awareness and foster collaboration.

---

[68] https://airiam.com/auto-dealerships-cybersecurity/.

Facilitating External Communication and Coordination

- Customers and partners: Transparency and timely communication are paramount when informing affected customers and business partners about the incident. Car dealerships should promptly notify them of the breach, its potential impact, and the actions to address the situation. Regular updates on progress and mitigation efforts help maintain trust and confidence.[69]
- Regulatory authorities: Compliance with data protection regulations is a legal obligation for car dealerships. In the event of a data breach, the dealership must promptly notify relevant regulatory bodies, such as the FTC, to adhere to legal requirements and avoid potential penalties.[70]
- Law enforcement: Car dealerships should collaborate with law enforcement agencies, such as local police or the FBI, to report cyber incidents, share relevant evidence, and seek assistance in investigating and prosecuting cybercriminals. Timely engagement with law enforcement can enhance the chances of apprehending the perpetrators.[71]
- Legal counsel: Early engagement of legal counsel is crucial to understanding the legal obligations, privacy implications, and potential liabilities associated with the incident. Legal counsel can guide reporting requirements, customer notification, and liability considerations.[72]

Emphasizing Collaboration with Stakeholders

- Third-party service providers: Car dealerships should proactively engage with third-party service providers, such as cybersecurity firms and IT vendors, to effectively leverage their expertise and resources in addressing the incident.

---

[69] https://ideas.repec.org/a/aza/jdpp00/y2019v2i4p362-367.html.
[70] https://arcticwolf.com/resources/blog/car-dealerships-dealers-must-bolster-data-security-under-new-ftc-rule/.
[71] http://www.forvis.com/article/2022/07/dealerships-comply-ftc-data-breach-safeguards.
[72] https://ideas.repec.org/a/aza/jdpp00/y2019v2i4p362-367.html.

- Insurance carriers: Involving insurance carriers early in the incident response process is essential to determine the extent of coverage and financial support available for response and recovery efforts.
- Internal teams: Collaboration with internal teams, such as human resources and public relations, is crucial during a cyber incident. Human resources can address workforce concerns and personnel-related issues, while the public relations team can manage the dealership's image and reputation.

Maintaining Confidentiality and Managing Public Relations

Confidentiality

During a cyber incident, maintaining confidentiality is essential to preserve the investigation's integrity and protect sensitive information. Dealerships should establish clear guidelines on handling media inquiries and communications with external parties to prevent the inadvertent disclosure of sensitive information.[73]

Public Relations Strategy

Car dealerships should have a well-defined public relations strategy to manage the message conveyed to the media and the public. Designated spokespersons should communicate consistent and accurate information, and a central communication hub should oversee all media interactions.

Transparency and Reassurance

While maintaining confidentiality, the dealership should be transparent with customers and stakeholders about the incident, the actions to address it, and the steps to prevent future incidents. Providing reassurance demonstrates the dealership's commitment to safeguarding customer data.

Formalizing the Incident Response Team Activation Process

Activating the incident response team is critical in effectively responding to a security incident. Car dealerships should formalize the incident response

---

[73] https://www.ftc.gov/system/files/documents/plain-language/560a_data_breach_response_guide_for_business.pdf.

team's activation process to ensure a swift and coordinated response. It involves designating a point person for external communication, creating criteria for law enforcement involvement, and developing communication templates for customer outreach.[74]

Activation Process

Contacting the Security Operations Center

Any employee suspecting a security incident should immediately contact the organization's security operations center (SOC) or other designated twenty-four/seven monitoring point. The SOC will conduct a standard triage process to assess the event's severity.

Alerting Mechanism

Car dealerships should consider using alerting mechanisms like PagerDuty or Opsgenie to expedite the activation process. These platforms manage on-call schedules and trigger alerts through multiple communication channels, promptly ensuring a faster response by convening the incident response team.

Designating a Point Person for External Communication

- Crisis communication role: As soon as a security incident is identified, external stakeholders, including customers, media, regulators, and others, will seek information. To provide a clear and consistent message across communication channels, the incident response team should designate a communication role responsible for external communication and updates.[75]
- Coordinated response: The designated communication role ensures that all external communications are consistent and coordinated. This role will be responsible for crafting communication messages, addressing inquiries from external stakeholders, and controlling rumors to maintain the organization's reputation during the incident.[76]

---

[74] https://securityintelligence.com/posts/marketing-public-relations-incident-response/.
[75] https://leb.fbi.gov/articles/featured-articles/social-media-establishing-criteria-for-law-enforcement-use.
[76] https://leb.fbi.gov/articles/featured-articles/social-media-establishing-criteria-for-law-enforcement-use.

Creating Criteria for Law Enforcement Involvement

- Critical decision points: Incident response teams face crucial decisions regarding involving law enforcement and when to notify them. The incident response communication plan should outline clear criteria for determining when law enforcement should be notified and identify the team member with the authority to make that decision.
- Internal notifications: The team should consult with executive leadership and legal counsel before involving law enforcement. The plan should specify the internal notifications that need to take place before engaging law enforcement.

Developing Communication Templates for Customer Outreach:

Importance of Communication Templates: Many security incidents require communication with customers or the public. Communication templates play a vital role in providing a consistent and well-crafted message. They save time and ensure that the incident response team can quickly and effectively communicate with stakeholders.

- Preapproved templates: The incident response communication plan should include preapproved communication templates for various types of incidents. These templates should be developed in advance, involving input from relevant stakeholders, such as account managers, executives, legal counsel, and PR experts.
- Flexibility in templates: While templates provide a framework, they should also allow customization to address the specific incident's nuances. The incident response team can adapt the templates to fill in relevant details and make necessary adjustments.

Transparency, confidentiality, and timely communication foster trust among customers and stakeholders, preserving the dealership's reputation and mitigating the impact of cyber incidents. By implementing a proactive and collaborative approach to communication and coordination, car dealerships can effectively navigate cybersecurity challenges and protect their operations and customers from evolving cyber threats.

C. BUSINESS CONTINUITY PLANNING AND RECOVERY MEASURES FOR CAR DEALERSHIPS IN CYBERSECURITY INCIDENTS

Car dealerships rely heavily on computer systems, networks, and data to manage their operations efficiently and serve customers effectively. However, the increasing sophistication of cyber threats poses significant risks to the automotive industry. Cybersecurity incidents, such as data breaches, ransomware attacks, and denial-of-service (DoS) attacks, can disrupt dealership operations, compromise customer information, and damage the dealership's reputation. To ensure business continuity and minimize downtime in the face of such incidents, car dealerships must have a comprehensive business continuity plan (BCP) and effective recovery measures in place.

Understanding Business Continuity Planning

Business continuity planning is a proactive approach to identifying potential risks and developing strategies to maintain essential operations during and after a cybersecurity incident. It involves assessing potential threats, defining critical business functions, and implementing measures to ensure continuity during disruptions. Business continuity planning is paramount for car dealerships to ensure uninterrupted services to customers, secure sensitive data, and protect the dealership's reputation.[77]

Risk Assessment

The first step in business continuity planning is a thorough risk assessment. Car dealerships must identify cybersecurity threats and vulnerabilities in their IT systems, networks, and processes. This assessment should include a comprehensive review of the dealership's digital assets, such as customer data, financial records, inventory management systems, and communication channels.

---

[77] https://digitaldealer.com/dealer-ops-leadership/four-cybersecurity-basics-must-haves-auto-dealerships/.

Business Impact Analysis

Once potential risks are identified, a business impact analysis (BIA) helps prioritize critical business functions and processes. This analysis considers the potential consequences of disruptions and helps allocate resources and prioritize recovery efforts accordingly. For example, ensuring customer data security and maintaining core sales and service operations might be designated as top priorities.

Continuity Strategies

Based on the BIA results, car dealerships can develop continuity strategies tailored to their unique requirements. These strategies may include redundant systems, backup and recovery procedures, disaster recovery plans, and communication protocols.[78]

Implementing Effective Backup and Recovery Procedures

Data is the lifeblood of any car dealership, and protecting it from loss or corruption is paramount. Implementing robust backup and recovery procedures ensures business continuity during a cybersecurity incident.

Regular Data Backups

Car dealerships should establish a reliable data backup strategy involving frequent critical data backups. Regular backups ensure that the most up-to-date information is available for recovery in case of a data breach or system failure.

On-Site and Off-Site Storage

Data backups should be stored on-site and off-site to safeguard data from physical disasters and cyberattacks. On-site backups provide quick access to data for recovery, while off-site backups act as a fail-safe in case the on-site data is compromised.

---

[78] https://mcmcpa.com/ftc-cyber-regulation-changes-for-auto-dealerships/.

Data Recovery Testing

More than having data backups is required; regular testing of the data recovery process is crucial. Car dealerships should conduct periodic data recovery tests to verify the accessibility and integrity of backup data. Testing helps identify potential issues and ensures a smooth recovery process when needed.

Encryption and Security

To protect backup data from unauthorized access, encryption should be employed. Access controls and authentication measures should also be applied to restrict access to backup data only to authorized personnel.

Incorporating Redundant Systems

Redundancy is a crucial component of business continuity planning. Having redundant systems and infrastructure ensures critical operations can continue even if primary systems fail.

Redundant Hardware and Infrastructure

Car dealerships should consider deploying redundant servers, network equipment, and power sources to ensure continuous operations. Redundancy minimizes the impact of hardware failures and network outages.

Failover Mechanisms

Implementing failover mechanisms allows automatic switching to redundant systems if the primary system becomes unavailable. It ensures seamless transitions and minimal disruption to business operations.

Developing Comprehensive Disaster Recovery Plans

Disaster recovery plans (DRPs) are essential components of business continuity planning. These plans outline the steps to be taken during and after a cybersecurity incident to recover operations and restore normalcy.

Incident-Specific Plans

Car dealerships should develop disaster recovery plans that address specific cybersecurity incidents. These plans should consider data breaches, ransomware attacks, DoS attacks, and other potential threats.

Roles and Responsibilities

Each incident response team member should have clearly defined roles and responsibilities outlined in the disaster recovery plans. Further, it ensures a coordinated response and efficient execution of recovery measures.

Communication and Notification

Effective communication is crucial during a cybersecurity incident. Car dealerships should have communication protocols to notify relevant stakeholders, including employees, customers, vendors, and regulatory authorities. Timely and accurate communication helps manage the situation and maintain trust with stakeholders.

Regular Testing and Updating

Business continuity and disaster recovery plans should be regularly tested and updated to ensure their effectiveness in real-world scenarios.

Testing Business Continuity Plans

Regular business continuity and disaster recovery plan testing are essential to verify their efficacy. Testing helps identify weaknesses, refine procedures, and train employees on their roles during an incident.[79]

Tabletop Exercises

Conducting tabletop exercises allows the incident response team to simulate various cybersecurity incidents and practice their response strategies. These exercises help assess the team's preparedness and improve decision-making capabilities.

---

[79] https://www.vistainfosec.com/blog/testing-the-business-continuity-plan/.

Plan Updates

The cybersecurity landscape is constantly evolving, and business continuity plans should be regularly updated to address emerging threats, technological advancements, and changes in the dealership's operations. Regular plan updates ensure the dealership remains resilient and prepared against evolving cyber threats.

Business continuity planning and effective recovery measures are critical for car dealerships to minimize downtime and ensure seamless operations during cybersecurity incidents. A well-designed business continuity plan involves understanding potential risks, prioritizing critical functions, and implementing redundancy and recovery strategies. Data backups, redundant systems, and comprehensive disaster recovery plans form the foundation of a robust business continuity strategy. Regular testing and updates ensure that car dealerships remain resilient and prepared in the face of evolving cyber threats.[80] By prioritizing business continuity planning, car dealerships can safeguard their reputation, maintain customer trust, and protect their bottom line.

---

[80] https://www.diligent.com/insights/business-continuity/bcp-maintenance/.

CHAPTER 8

VENDOR RISK MANAGEMENT: SECURING THIRD-PARTY RELATIONSHIPS

A. ASSESSING CYBERSECURITY PRACTICES OF THIRD-PARTY VENDORS AND SUPPLIERS

Car dealerships often rely on third-party vendors and suppliers to enhance their operations, provide specialized services, and support various aspects of their business. While these collaborations can bring valuable benefits, they also introduce potential cybersecurity risks. Third-party vendors may have access to sensitive customer data, critical systems, or networks, making them potential targets for cyberattacks. To ensure the security and integrity of dealership operations, it is essential to assess the cybersecurity practices of third-party vendors and suppliers.

Understanding the Risks of Third-Party Relationships

Third-party vendors and suppliers can be significant sources of cybersecurity vulnerabilities for car dealerships. When engaging with external entities, car dealerships must be aware of the following potential risks:

Data Breaches

Third-party vendors often handle sensitive customer information, financial records, and other confidential data on behalf of car dealerships. A data breach at a vendor's end can expose this sensitive information, causing significant reputational damage and legal liabilities.

Supply Chain Attacks

Attackers may target vulnerabilities within the supply chain to gain unauthorized access to the dealership's network or systems. Weak security practices by third-party vendors could serve as an entry point for cybercriminals.[81]

---

[81] https://nvlpubs.nist.gov/nistpubs/ir/2021/NIST.IR.8276.pdf.

Service Disruptions

Ransomware attacks or other cyber incidents impacting vendors can disrupt the services they provide to the dealership. It can result in operational disruptions and financial losses.

Regulatory Compliance

Car dealerships may be held accountable for the actions of their third-party vendors, especially when it comes to compliance with data protection and privacy regulations. Please assess vendor cybersecurity practices to avoid regulatory noncompliance.

Conducting Due Diligence and Assessments:

To mitigate the cybersecurity risks associated with third-party relationships, car dealerships must conduct thorough due diligence and assessments before engaging with vendors and suppliers. The goal is to evaluate the vendor's cybersecurity posture and ensure adequate security measures are in place to protect the dealership's data and systems.

Assessment Criteria

Developing comprehensive assessment criteria is essential to effectively consider third-party vendors' cybersecurity practices. These criteria may include the following:

- Security policies and procedures: Assess the vendor's security policies, procedures, and practices related to data protection, access controls, incident response, and employee training.
- Data handling practices: Understand how the vendor handles and protects sensitive data in transit and at rest. Ensure they follow industry best practices for data encryption and storage.
- Security controls: Evaluate the vendor's technical security controls, such as firewalls, intrusion detection systems, antivirus solutions, and vulnerability management practices.
- Incident response capabilities: Determine the vendor's incident response capabilities, including their ability to detect, contain, and respond to cybersecurity incidents.

- Compliance and certifications: Check if the vendor complies with relevant data protection regulations and industry standards and holds any cybersecurity certifications.

Assessment Techniques

Car dealerships can use various assessment techniques to evaluate the cybersecurity practices of third-party vendors, such as the following:

- Questionnaires: Distribute cybersecurity questionnaires to vendors to gather information about their security practices and controls. These questionnaires can cover various aspects of cybersecurity, such as data protection measures, access controls, and incident response protocols.
- On-site visits: Conduct on-site visits to vendors' facilities to observe their security measures firsthand and evaluate their physical security. This includes assessing the access controls to their data centers, the presence of surveillance cameras, and other physical security measures.
- Penetration testing: Engage third-party cybersecurity firms to conduct penetration tests on vendors' networks and systems to identify potential vulnerabilities. Penetration testing simulates real-world cyberattacks to identify weaknesses and assess the vendor's ability to withstand attacks.
- Reference checks: Speak with other clients or companies that have worked with the vendor to understand their experiences and security concerns. These references can provide valuable insights into the vendor's track record and commitment to cybersecurity.[82]
- Audits and certifications: Review the results of any independent security audits or certifications the vendor has undergone. Certifications, such as ISO 27001 or SOC 2, can indicate that the vendor has met specific security standards.

---

[82] https://blog.rsisecurity.com/your-third-party-cyber-risk-assessment-checklist/.

Ongoing Monitoring

Vendor risk management is an ongoing process that extends beyond the initial assessment. Car dealerships should establish a method for continuously monitoring third-party vendors to ensure they maintain the required security standards over time. It can include periodic reassessments, reviewing new audits or certification results, and tracking for any security incidents or breaches involving the vendor.

Establishing Contractual Obligations

As part of the vendor risk management process, car dealerships should include specific cybersecurity requirements in their contracts with third-party vendors. These contractual obligations may include the following:

- Data protection and confidentiality: Vendors should be contractually obligated to protect the dealership's data and maintain its confidentiality. This includes requirements for data encryption, secure data storage, and limitations on data access.
- Incident reporting and response: Vendors should be required to promptly report any cybersecurity incidents or data breaches to the dealership. Additionally, the contract should outline the vendor's responsibilities for incident response and investigation cooperation.
- Compliance with regulations: The contract should specify that the vendor must comply with all applicable data protection and privacy regulations, including those related to the dealership's industry.
- Termination and transition: The contract should outline the procedures for termination of the relationship in case of a cybersecurity breach or failure to meet security requirements. It should also address the secure transition of data and services to another vendor if necessary.

Assessing the cybersecurity practices of third-party vendors and suppliers is critical for car dealerships to manage and mitigate potential cybersecurity risks. By conducting due diligence, utilizing appropriate assessment techniques, and establishing clear contractual obligations, car dealerships can make informed decisions about their vendor relationships and ensure that their partners meet adequate security standards.

B. ESTABLISHING SECURITY STANDARDS AND REQUIREMENTS IN VENDOR CONTRACTS

Car dealerships must prioritize cybersecurity and data protection when engaging with third-party vendors. Establishing security standards and requirements in vendor contracts is crucial to safeguarding sensitive information, maintaining customer trust, and mitigating potential cyber risks. By incorporating cybersecurity clauses, data protection obligations, and incident response expectations into vendor contracts, car dealerships can ensure that their partners adhere to adequate security practices. This chapter guides how to include essential security provisions in vendor contracts and emphasizes the significance of ongoing monitoring and auditing to ensure vendor compliance.

Cybersecurity Clauses in Vendor Contracts

To enforce a strong security posture among vendors, car dealerships should include cybersecurity clauses in their contracts. Vendors must follow these clauses as contractual obligations to protect the dealership's data and systems.[83] Key cybersecurity clauses may consist of the following:

Information Security Responsibility

The contract should explicitly state that the vendor is responsible for maintaining the security and confidentiality of all dealership data and information entrusted to them. It should outline the specific security measures and controls the vendor must implement to protect this data.

Access Controls and Authentication

Vendors must adhere to strict access controls and authentication mechanisms to ensure that only authorized personnel can access sensitive data. It includes implementing strong password policies, multifactor authentication, and role-based access controls.

---

[83] https://www.aspentechpolicyhub.org/wp-content/uploads/2020/06/Vendor-Cybersecurity-Contract-Language.pdf.

Data Encryption

The contract should require the vendor to encrypt all sensitive data, both in transit and at rest, to protect it from unauthorized access or disclosure.

Security Incident Reporting

Vendors should be contractually obligated to promptly report any security incidents or data breaches to the car dealership. This enables the dealership to respond quickly and effectively to any cybersecurity threats.

Subcontractor Security

Suppose the vendor engages subcontractors or third parties to provide services. In that case, the contract should ensure that these entities meet the same cybersecurity and data protection standards as the primary vendor.

Data Protection Obligations

Data protection is critical to vendor contracts, primarily when vendors handle sensitive customer information. Car dealerships should include data protection obligations to ensure the vendor's compliance with relevant data protection laws and regulations. Fundamental data protection obligations may consist of the following:

Data Processing and Use

The contract should specify the purposes for which the vendor can process the dealership's data. It should also prohibit the vendor from using the data for any other purposes without the dealership's explicit consent.

Data Retention and Deletion

Vendors should only retain the dealership's data for as long as necessary to fulfill the agreed-upon services. The contract should outline data retention periods and require the vendor to delete or return the data upon contract termination.

Data Transfer Restrictions

If the vendor transfers data to jurisdictions outside the dealership's country, the contract should address how the vendor ensures adequate data protection in those jurisdictions.

Employee Training and Awareness

Vendors should train their employees on data protection principles and cybersecurity best practices. The contract should require the vendor to demonstrate its commitment to employee training and awareness.

Incident Response Expectations

A well-defined incident response plan is crucial for timely and effective action in a cybersecurity incident or data breach. The contract should set clear expectations for incident response, including the following:

Incident Notification

Vendors must promptly notify the car dealership of any cybersecurity incidents or data breaches that may impact the dealership's data or systems.

Incident Investigation and Cooperation

The contract should outline the vendor's responsibilities for cooperating with the dealership's incident response team during the investigation and resolution.

Remediation and Mitigation

Vendors should take immediate remediation and mitigation actions to contain the incident and prevent further damage or data loss.

Forensic Analysis

The contract may include provisions for engaging third-party forensic experts to analyze the incident if necessary.

Ongoing Monitoring and Auditing of Vendor Compliance

Establishing security standards and requirements in vendor contracts is just the first step. Car dealerships must continuously monitor and audit vendor compliance to ensure security measures remain practical and up to date. Critical aspects of ongoing monitoring and auditing include the following:

Periodic Assessments

Conduct periodic assessments of vendors' security practices and controls to verify compliance with contractual obligations. It may involve using questionnaires, on-site visits, or third-party audits.

Incident Reporting and Response Testing

Regularly test vendors' incident reporting and response capabilities through simulated scenarios. It helps identify any weaknesses in their incident management processes.

Compliance with Data Protection Regulations

Monitor vendors' compliance with data protection regulations and industry standards to ensure they keep pace with evolving cybersecurity requirements.

Review of Security Controls

Regularly review the effectiveness of vendors' security controls and ensure they align with industry best practices.

Contractual Remedies

Establish contractual remedies in case of vendor noncompliance with security standards. These may include the right to terminate the contract or impose penalties for serious security breaches.

C. ONGOING MONITORING AND AUDITS TO ENSURE COMPLIANCE AND MITIGATE RISKS

Effective vendor risk management goes beyond establishing security standards in vendor contracts. Car dealerships must implement ongoing monitoring and audits to ensure third-party vendors comply with cybersecurity requirements and proactively mitigate potential risks. Continuous evaluation through audits, vulnerability assessments, and penetration testing enables car dealerships to identify vulnerabilities and security gaps, allowing for prompt remediation and strengthening of their overall cybersecurity posture. This chapter explores the importance of ongoing monitoring and audits in vendor risk management and provides best practices for conducting these assessments.

Importance of Ongoing Monitoring and Audits

Regular monitoring and audits are essential to a robust vendor risk management program. They serve several critical purposes, including the following:

Risk Mitigation

Ongoing monitoring and audits allow car dealerships to identify and address potential cybersecurity risks vendors pose. By promptly detecting vulnerabilities or noncompliance, dealerships can take corrective actions to mitigate these risks before they escalate.

Compliance Verification

Monitoring and audits verify that vendors meet the security standards outlined in their contracts. This ensures that vendors adhere to agreed-upon data protection and incident response obligations.

Security Incident Detection

Continuous monitoring helps identify security incidents or data breaches promptly. Rapid detection enables quick response and containment, minimizing the impact of the incident on the dealership's operations and reputation.

Proactive Response

Regular audits provide valuable insights into the effectiveness of security controls and practices. Armed with this information, car dealerships can proactively enhance their cybersecurity defenses to stay ahead of emerging threats.

Best Practices for Conducting Regular Audits

To ensure comprehensive vendor risk management, car dealerships should adopt the following best practices for conducting regular audits:

Establish Audit Schedule

Develop a clear audit schedule to ensure that all vendors are audited periodically. The frequency of audits may vary based on the level of risk associated with each vendor and the sensitivity of the data they handle.

Use Risk-Based Approach

Prioritize vendors based on risk levels to focus efforts on vendors with a higher potential impact on the dealership's operations and data security.

Utilize Questionnaires and Surveys

Use questionnaires and surveys to gather vendor information about security practices, controls, and compliance status. It allows the dealership to assess vendor cybersecurity posture efficiently.

Conduct On-Site Visits

In addition to questionnaires, consider conducting on-site visits to vendors' facilities. On-site visits provide an opportunity to observe their security infrastructure and practices firsthand.

Engage Third-Party Auditors

Consider engaging third-party auditors to conduct independent audits of vendors. Third-party auditors bring impartiality and expertise to the assessment process, providing a more objective evaluation.

Review Incident Response Preparedness

Assess vendors' incident response capabilities to ensure they can effectively detect, contain, and respond to security incidents.

Vulnerability Assessments and Penetration Testing

In addition to audits, car dealerships should regularly perform vulnerability assessments and penetration testing to identify potential weaknesses in both their systems and their vendors. These assessments help uncover vulnerabilities before malicious actors can exploit them. Best practices for vulnerability assessments and penetration testing include the following:

Internal and External Vulnerability Scanning

Perform regular internal and external vulnerability scanning of the dealership's networks, systems, and applications. Similarly, request vendors to conduct vulnerability assessments on their systems.

Penetration Testing

Conduct periodic penetration testing to simulate real-world cyberattacks and assess the resilience of the dealership's and vendors' defenses.

Red Team Assessments

Consider red team assessments, where ethical hackers simulate advanced threats to identify potential security controls and response capabilities gaps.

Collaborative Approaches

Collaborate with vendors to share findings from vulnerability assessments and penetration testing. It encourages a shared responsibility for security and fosters a collaborative approach to risk mitigation.

Steps to Take When Vulnerabilities or Breaches Are Discovered

When monitoring, audits, or assessments uncover vulnerabilities or security incidents, it is essential to take prompt and decisive action. The following steps should be taken when vulnerabilities or breaches are discovered:

1. Incident response protocol: Activate the incident response protocol outlined in the vendor contract and the dealership's incident response plan.
2. Notification: Notify the vendor of the identified vulnerabilities or breaches and request immediate remediation and containment measures.
3. Remediation and mitigation: Work collaboratively with the vendor to remediate the identified vulnerabilities or mitigate the breach's impact.
4. Follow-up audit: Conduct a follow-up audit to verify that the vendor has addressed the identified issues effectively.
5. Escalation: If the vendor fails to address the vulnerabilities or respond adequately to the breach, consider escalating the matter to higher management or legal counsel, as outlined in the vendor contract.
6. Decision-making: Based on the severity of the vulnerabilities or breach and the vendor's response, evaluate whether the partnership with the vendor should continue or if additional measures are necessary to protect the dealership's interests.

Ongoing monitoring and audits are indispensable components of a robust vendor risk management program. Car dealerships can identify potential risks, maintain compliance, and proactively address security weaknesses by continually evaluating vendor cybersecurity practices through audits, vulnerability assessments, and penetration testing. Timely detection of vulnerabilities and incidents enables swift response and mitigation, safeguarding sensitive data and ensuring the dealership's and its vendors' overall cybersecurity resilience. Continuous improvement and vigilance in vendor risk management are fundamental to building a secure and trusted ecosystem of third-party partnerships in the automotive industry.

CHAPTER 9

EMPLOYEE TRAINING AND AWARENESS: BUILDING A CYBERSECURITY CULTURE IN DEALERSHIPS

A. IMPORTANCE OF CYBERSECURITY TRAINING FOR DEALERSHIP EMPLOYEES

Cybersecurity threats have become a pervasive concern for car dealerships. With increasing cyberattacks and data breaches targeting businesses of all sizes, it has become crucial for dealerships to prioritize cybersecurity training for their employees. Human error remains one of the most significant vulnerabilities in any organization's cybersecurity defense. Therefore, fostering a security-conscious workforce is essential in building a robust cybersecurity culture that safeguards sensitive data, customer information, and the dealership's reputation. This chapter highlights the critical role of employee training in cultivating a cybersecurity culture within car dealerships. It emphasizes the employees' position as the first line of defense against cyber threats.

The Potential Impact of Human Error

Despite having sophisticated cybersecurity technologies and protocols, employees can unintentionally introduce vulnerabilities through human error. Common examples include falling victim to phishing emails, using weak passwords, accessing insecure Wi-Fi networks, or mishandling sensitive data. Cybercriminals often exploit these human weaknesses as an entry point into the dealership's network. A single employee's mistake can lead to significant consequences, including data breaches, financial losses, legal ramifications, and damage to the dealership's reputation.[84]

Building a Security-Conscious Workforce

Training employees to recognize and respond effectively to cybersecurity threats is paramount in creating a security-conscious workforce. The goal is to empower employees with the knowledge and skills needed to identify and avoid potential risks, ensuring they play an active role in maintaining the dealership's cybersecurity defenses.[85]

---

[84] https://www.makeuseof.com/importance-cybersecurity-training-employees/.
[85] https://www.cisa.gov/sites/default/files/publications/Cyber%20Essentials%20 Toolkit%202%2020200701.pdf.

Understanding Cyber Threats

Begin training with an overview of the cybersecurity landscape, the various cyber threats, and their potential impact on the dealership. Explain the concept of social engineering and how cybercriminals exploit human vulnerabilities to gain unauthorized access to systems and data.

Recognizing Phishing Attacks

Phishing attacks remain one of the most prevalent methods cybercriminals use to infiltrate organizations. Train employees to identify phishing emails, fake web sites, and suspicious links. Teach them to verify the authenticity of emails, especially those requesting sensitive information or financial transactions.

Password Management

Emphasize the importance of strong password practices, such as using unique and complex passwords for each account, enabling multifactor authentication, and avoiding the use of easily guessable information.

Secure Wi-Fi Usage

Educate employees about the risks of using unsecured public Wi-Fi networks and encourage them to use virtual private networks (VPNs) when accessing company resources remotely.

Data Handling and Privacy

Train employees on proper data handling and privacy practices, including secure document disposal, securing physical files, and following data protection regulations, such as the General Data Protection Regulation and the California Consumer Privacy Act.[86]

---

[86] https://link.springer.com/chapter/10.1007/978-3-642-28920-0_4.

Mobile Device Security

With the increasing use of mobile devices for work-related tasks, educate employees on security best practices, such as enabling device passcodes, keeping software up to date, and avoiding public charging stations.

Employees as the First Line of Defense

Employees are the dealership's first line of defense against cyber threats. The dealership strengthens its overall security posture by instilling a cybersecurity mindset in employees. Encourage employees to do the following:

Report Suspicious Activity

Promote a culture where employees feel comfortable promptly reporting suspicious emails, messages, or incidents to the IT or security team.

Stay Informed

Encourage employees to stay informed about cybersecurity threats and best practices by attending regular training sessions, workshops, and webinars.

Be Diligent in Social Media

Train employees on the risks associated with oversharing on social media platforms and the potential for social engineering attacks.

Maintain Cyber Hygiene

Reinforce the importance of maintaining cyber hygiene by regularly updating software, using firewalls, and avoiding unauthorized software downloads.

Conduct Phishing Simulations

Periodically conduct phishing simulations to test employees' ability to identify phishing attempts and provide feedback and additional training as needed.

Training for dealership employees is integral to building a strong cybersecurity culture and protecting sensitive data and critical assets. Recognizing the potential impact of human error, dealerships must invest in comprehensive training programs that educate employees about cyber threats, teach them how to recognize and respond to potential risks and foster a security-conscious mindset. By empowering employees to be proactive defenders against cyber threats, car dealerships can establish a united front in safeguarding their digital assets, customer information, and overall reputation. Employee training is not a one-time endeavor; it requires ongoing reinforcement and adaptation to address emerging threats and evolving cybersecurity challenges. With a security-conscious workforce, car dealerships can significantly strengthen their cybersecurity defenses and create a safer digital environment for their operations and customers.

B. STRATEGIES FOR PROMOTING A SECURITY-CONSCIOUS CULTURE AND EMPLOYEE ENGAGEMENT

Building a security-conscious culture within car dealerships requires a comprehensive and detailed approach encompassing various strategies and best practices. This section will delve deeper into each strategy, providing more detailed insights on effectively promoting cybersecurity awareness and employee engagement.

Leadership Commitment

Secure Executive Buy-In

To establish a security-conscious culture, dealership leaders must demonstrate a genuine commitment to cybersecurity. Executives should actively participate in cybersecurity initiatives, attend training sessions, and engage with the cybersecurity team to understand the challenges and risks. By leading by example, executives set the tone for the entire organization.

Create a Cybersecurity Committee

Forming a cybersecurity committee comprising representatives from different departments can help ensure cross-functional collaboration and support for security initiatives. This committee can regularly meet to discuss cybersecurity issues, propose improvements, and align security strategies with overall business goals.[87]

Align Cybersecurity Goals with Business Objectives

Integrating cybersecurity objectives with the organization's overall business goals highlights its importance and demonstrates the tangible impact of cybersecurity on the dealership's success. For example, emphasizing the protection of customer data aligns with the dealership's commitment to customer trust and satisfaction.

Encourage Reporting and Transparency

Dealership leaders should foster an environment where employees feel comfortable reporting security incidents without fear of retribution. Transparent communication about incidents and their resolutions helps employees understand the real-world consequences of cyber threats and reinforces the importance of cybersecurity in the organization.

Effective Communication

Tailored Messaging

Customize cybersecurity messages to resonate with various employee groups. For example, sales staff may be more interested in protecting customer data and ensuring smooth transactions, while IT staff may focus on network security and system vulnerabilities. Tailoring messages ensures employees understand how cybersecurity relates to their roles and responsibilities.

Storytelling and Case Studies

Use real-world examples and case studies of cyber incidents to emphasize the relevance of cybersecurity and its potential impact on the dealership's reputation and customer trust. Humanizing cybersecurity incidents through storytelling can make the risks more tangible and relatable to employees.

---

[87] https://www.forbes.com/sites/forbesbusinesscouncil/2021/05/27/the-importance-of-a-strong-security-culture-and-how-to-build-one/.

Regular Newsletters and Updates

Send regular newsletters or updates on the latest cybersecurity threats, best practices, and success stories to keep employees informed and engaged.[88] Providing relevant and timely information helps employees stay vigilant and prepared to handle potential threats.

Continuous Training

Role-Based Training

Tailor training programs address employees' unique cybersecurity challenges in different roles, such as sales representatives, finance personnel, or IT administrators. Role-based training ensures that employees receive relevant and practical cybersecurity guidance directly impacting their daily tasks.

Hands-On Workshops and Simulations

Organize hands-on workshops and simulations that allow employees to practice responding to real-world cyber incidents, improving their incident response skills. Interactive exercises provide practical experience and help employees develop confidence in handling security-related situations.

Continuous Learning Platforms

Provide employees access to online learning platforms offering cybersecurity courses and certifications to enhance their knowledge and skills. Offering self-paced learning opportunities empowers employees to take ownership of their cybersecurity education.

Security Awareness Assessment

Conduct regular security awareness assessments to gauge training programs' effectiveness and identify improvement areas. These assessments can take the form of quizzes, mock phishing campaigns, or practical scenarios to test employees' knowledge and awareness.[89]

---

[88] https://techbeacon.com/security/6-ways-develop-security-culture-top-bottom.
[89] https://www.npsa.gov.uk/security-culture.

Employee Engagement Methods

Gamification

Introduce gamified elements like quizzes, competitions, and leaderboards to make cybersecurity training more engaging and enjoyable. Gamification encourages healthy competition among employees and motivates them to participate in training activities actively.[90]

Recognition Programs

Implement recognition programs publicly acknowledging employees demonstrating exceptional cybersecurity practices, encouraging others to follow suit. Recognition can be awards, certificates, or spotlights in newsletters or company meetings.

Security Ambassador Program

Create a security ambassador program where employees can volunteer to become cybersecurity champions, promoting best practices and serving as mentors to their peers. Ambassadors act as role models and advocates for cybersecurity awareness.

Cybersecurity Challenges

Organize periodic cybersecurity challenges or "capture the flag" events where employees can test their skills and compete against each other in a friendly environment. These challenges promote teamwork and problem-solving while reinforcing cybersecurity concepts.[91]

Ongoing Awareness Campaigns

Monthly Themes

Devote each month to a specific cybersecurity theme and organize related activities, training sessions, and awareness campaigns. Themes could

---

[90] https://csrc.nist.gov/CSRC/media/Events/Federal-Information-Systems-Security-Educators-As/documents/9.pdf.

[91] https://journals.sagepub.com/doi/pdf/10.1177/21582440211000049.

include password security, phishing awareness, mobile device security, or data protection.

Phishing Campaigns

Conduct simulated phishing campaigns to educate employees on the dangers of phishing and reinforce the importance of vigilance. Simulated phishing exercises provide valuable feedback on employees' susceptibility to social engineering attacks.

Cybersecurity Bulletin Boards

Set up bulletin boards with cybersecurity tips, best practices, and the latest threat information in common areas to remind employees regularly. Visual cues can serve as constant reminders of the dealership's commitment to cybersecurity.

Rewards and Incentives

Offer rewards or incentives for employees actively participating in cybersecurity awareness programs or successfully identifying and reporting potential threats. Rewards can range from small tokens of appreciation to more significant incentives for exceptional contributions to security.

Creating a security-conscious culture and engaging employees in cybersecurity requires an ongoing and dedicated effort from dealership leaders and cybersecurity teams. By combining leadership commitment, effective communication, continuous training, employee engagement methods, and ongoing awareness campaigns, car dealerships can foster a proactive cybersecurity culture where employees understand the importance of cybersecurity and actively contribute to the dealership's overall security posture. With a well-informed and engaged workforce, car dealerships can significantly reduce their vulnerability to cyber threats, protect customer data, and ensure the continuity of their business operations. Embracing a security-conscious culture becomes a shared responsibility among employees, ultimately strengthening the dealership's ability to successfully navigate the evolving cybersecurity landscape.

C. CONDUCTING PHISHING SIMULATIONS AND AWARENESS CAMPAIGNS TO ENHANCE PREPAREDNESS

Conducting phishing simulations and awareness campaigns is essential to a comprehensive cybersecurity training program that enhances dealership preparedness against cyber threats. These initiatives are crucial in identifying vulnerabilities, raising employee awareness, and fostering a security-conscious culture within the organization.

Benefits of Phishing Simulations

Identifying vulnerabilities: Phishing simulations allow the dealership's cybersecurity team to assess the organization's susceptibility to social engineering attacks. By creating realistic phishing emails, the team can gauge how employees respond to suspicious messages, click on malicious links, or provide sensitive information. Identifying vulnerabilities enables targeted training to address specific weaknesses.

Raising Awareness

Phishing simulations serve as eye-opening experiences for employees, demonstrating the tactics cybercriminals use to exploit human error. When employees fall for simulated phishing attacks, it reinforces the importance of vigilance and the need for continuous cybersecurity training.

Realistic Practice

Phishing simulations provide a safe environment for employees to practice recognizing and responding to phishing attempts. This hands-on experience enables employees to develop the skills necessary to avoid falling victim to real phishing attacks.[92]

Metrics and Analytics

Phishing simulations generate valuable data and metrics, such as click-through rates, response times, and trends. These insights help measure

---

[92] https://www.breachlock.com/resources/blog/benefits-of-phishing-simulations/.

the effectiveness of awareness campaigns, identify trends, and track improvements over time.

Components of Phishing Awareness Campaigns

Training modules: Comprehensive phishing awareness campaigns include interactive training modules that educate employees about different types of phishing attacks, common red flags, and best practices for handling suspicious emails. The training should cover topics like recognizing phishing URLs, verifying sender authenticity, and reporting suspicious emails.

- Simulated phishing exercises: Phishing simulations should mimic real-world scenarios with varying degrees of difficulty and sophistication. The simulated emails should closely resemble common phishing attempts, such as urgent requests for password changes, fake invoice notifications, or bogus package delivery alerts.
- Post-simulation feedback: After conducting phishing simulations, provide prompt feedback to employees who click on phishing emails. This feedback should be constructive and emphasize the importance of remaining vigilant to prevent real security incidents.
- Rewards and incentives: To encourage participation and engagement, consider implementing a rewards system for employees demonstrating exemplary phishing awareness skills. Rewards can include gift cards, certificates of achievement, or recognition during company-wide meetings.[93]

Benefits of Awareness Campaigns

- Cultivating cybersecurity culture: Awareness campaigns build a security-conscious culture within the dealership. Employees are encouraged to proactively identify and report potential threats by consistently promoting cybersecurity as a shared responsibility.
- Consistent messaging: Awareness campaigns ensure that cybersecurity messages are consistently delivered to all employees.

---

[93] https://thedefenceworks.com/blog/the-benefits-of-using-phishing-simulations/.

Employees receive frequent reminders about cybersecurity best practices and ongoing threats through various communication channels.

- Reinforcing training: Awareness campaigns reinforce the lessons learned in cybersecurity training modules. Frequent exposure to cybersecurity-related content helps employees retain and apply the information in their daily activities.
- Building a security-conscious mindset: Continuous awareness campaigns help employees develop a security-conscious mindset, making them more cautious and vigilant in their interactions with emails, attachments, and external links.

Components of Awareness Campaigns

- Training modules: Similar to phishing awareness campaigns, general cybersecurity awareness campaigns include training modules that cover a wide range of cybersecurity topics, such as password security, data protection, and safe internet browsing.
- Posters and infographics: Display posters and infographics in common areas of the dealership, such as break rooms or hallways, to deliver concise and visually appealing cybersecurity tips and reminders.
- Newsletters: Include cybersecurity-related articles and updates in regular company newsletters. This approach ensures that cybersecurity remains a prominent topic and reinforces the organization's commitment to maintaining a secure environment.
- Webinars and workshops: Conduct webinars and workshops on specific cybersecurity topics to provide in-depth insights and engage employees in interactive discussions.
- Employee engagement: Encourage employees to actively participate in cybersecurity-related activities, such as quizzes, challenges, or feedback sessions. Involving employees in these initiatives fosters a sense of ownership in cybersecurity matters.

Conclusion

Conducting phishing simulations and implementing comprehensive awareness campaigns are vital to building a security-conscious culture within car dealerships. These initiatives are pivotal in enhancing dealership preparedness against cyber threats by identifying vulnerabilities, raising employee awareness, and fostering a proactive and vigilant workforce. With continuous training, engaging communication, and ongoing awareness campaigns, car dealerships can empower their employees to become the first line of defense against cyberattacks, protecting sensitive data and ensuring the dealership's overall cybersecurity resilience.

CHAPTER 10

NETWORK SECURITY: PROTECTING DEALERSHIP INFRASTRUCTURE AND DATA

A. IMPLEMENTING ROBUST NETWORK SECURITY MEASURES AND FIREWALLS

Implementing robust network security measures and firewalls is a foundational step in safeguarding sensitive information and customer data and ensuring the smooth functioning of dealership operations. This section dives deeper into the critical components of network security, shedding light on the significance of network segmentation, intrusion detection systems (IDS), and log monitoring. Additionally, it underscores the importance of conducting regular vulnerability assessments and applying timely security updates to maintain a strong and resilient defense against an ever-evolving array of cyber threats.

Network Segmentation

Network segmentation involves deliberately dividing the dealership's network into distinct zones or segments. Each segment is isolated from the others, creating an environment where a breach in one segment doesn't necessarily impact others. For example, sales and marketing departments can be isolated from financial systems and customer databases. This strategy significantly reduces the potential impact of a security breach.[94]

Benefits

- Minimized attack surface: By limiting lateral movement, even if one segment is compromised, the damage is contained, preventing the free movement of attackers across the network.
- Enhanced monitoring and control: Network administrators can better monitor and manage traffic within each segment, increasing the chances of identifying anomalies and unauthorized access attempts.
- Data protection: Isolating sensitive data in dedicated segments adds an extra layer of protection, preventing unauthorized access to critical information.

---

[94] https://www.eccouncil.org/cybersecurity-exchange/network-security/firewall-security-guide-concerns-capabilities-limitations/.

Firewalls

Firewalls act as the gatekeepers of a dealership's network, regulating incoming and outgoing traffic based on predefined security rules. By effectively filtering traffic, firewalls can prevent unauthorized access and block malicious data packets from entering the network.[95]

Benefits

- Access control: Firewalls enforce access controls, determining who can access the network and what actions are permissible.
- Threat prevention: Firewalls identify and block known attack patterns, reducing the risk of successful cyberattacks.
- Traffic monitoring: Firewall logs provide insights into network traffic, aiding in detecting potential breaches and unauthorized activities.

Intrusion Detection Systems

IDS are vigilant security tools that continuously monitor network traffic and system behavior for signs of unauthorized or malicious activities. They can be signature-based (identifying known attack patterns) or behavior-based (detecting anomalies compared to normal network behavior).[96]

Benefits

- Early threat detection: IDS can detect threats in real time, allowing for swift responses to potential security breaches.
- Alerting and reporting: When unusual activities are detected, IDS generates alerts for immediate attention and provide detailed reports for post-incident analysis.
- Forensic insights: IDS logs can offer valuable information for forensic investigation and analysis in the aftermath of a security incident.

---

[95] https://media.defense.gov/2022/Jun/15/2003018261/-1/-1/0/CTR_NSA_NETWORK_INFRASTRUCTURE_SECURITY_GUIDE_20220615.PDF.
[96] https://link.springer.com/article/10.1186/s42400-019-0038-7.

Log Monitoring

Effective log monitoring involves systematically collecting, analyzing, and reviewing logs generated by network devices, servers, and applications. These logs provide a detailed record of activities, allowing security teams to detect abnormal patterns and potential security breaches.

Benefits

- Anomaly detection: Log analysis can reveal irregular patterns, unauthorized access attempts, and suspicious activities that might go unnoticed otherwise.
- Real-time response: Prompt alerts triggered by unusual events enable security teams to respond quickly, mitigating potential threats.
- Compliance and auditing: Log monitoring is essential for meeting compliance requirements and demonstrating adherence to security standards.[97]

Regular Vulnerability Assessments

Vulnerability assessments involve systematic scanning of network assets and systems to identify potential weaknesses, misconfigurations, and outdated software. These assessments help organizations prioritize and address vulnerabilities before cybercriminals exploit them.

Benefits

- Proactive security: Vulnerability assessments allow organizations to identify weaknesses before exploiting them, reducing the risk of successful attacks.
- Informed decision-making: By understanding their vulnerabilities, dealerships can make informed decisions about security investments and improvements.

---

[97] https://www.frontiersin.org/articles/10.3389/fpubh.2021.788347/full.

- Patch management: Vulnerability assessments aid in identifying systems that require security patches, ensuring timely updates to mitigate risks.

Security Updates and Patches

Regularly updating operating systems, software applications, and network devices is essential to maintaining a secure network environment. Cybercriminals often target known vulnerabilities, making it imperative to apply security patches as soon as they are available.

Benefits

- Risk mitigation: Security updates close known vulnerabilities, reducing the likelihood of exploitation by cyberattackers.
- Protection against malware: Patches often address vulnerabilities that malware exploits to infiltrate systems, preventing potential breaches.
- Regulatory compliance: Many industries have regulatory requirements for maintaining up-to-date software, making patch management crucial for compliance.

Addressing the Need for Regular Vulnerability Assessments and Security Updates

Cyberattackers constantly seek to exploit vulnerabilities within an organization's network infrastructure and systems. Car dealerships are no exception, and the critical importance of conducting regular vulnerability assessments and applying timely security updates cannot be overstated. These practices are pivotal in maintaining a robust cybersecurity posture, reducing the attack surface, and safeguarding sensitive data against various cyber threats.

Vulnerability Assessments

Vulnerability assessments involve systematic and thorough scanning of the dealership's network, applications, and systems to identify potential security weaknesses and vulnerabilities. These assessments serve as a preemptive measure, allowing the organization to identify vulnerabilities before malicious actors can exploit them for unauthorized access or data breaches.

Benefits

Proactive Risk Management: Vulnerability assessments empower dealerships to take a proactive approach to risk management by identifying and addressing potential security gaps before attackers can capitalize on them.

Prioritizing Remediation: By quantifying the severity of vulnerabilities, dealerships can prioritize which issues to address first, focusing resources on the most critical areas.

Regulatory Compliance: Many industries have specific regulations that mandate regular vulnerability assessments to protect customer data and sensitive information.

Reduced Attack Surface: Addressing vulnerabilities narrows the potential points of entry for cyberattackers, making it more challenging for them to infiltrate the network.[98]

Security Updates and Patches

Security updates, often referred to as patches, are releases provided by software vendors to fix known vulnerabilities and address software bugs. Regularly applying these updates is essential for protecting software and systems against the latest threats. Cybercriminals frequently target known vulnerabilities, making it crucial for dealerships to stay ahead by implementing security updates promptly.

---

[98] https://citrixready.citrix.com/content/dam/ready/program/secure-remote-access-program/pdf-censornetmfaadvancednetscalerguide-web.pdf.

Benefits

- Vulnerability mitigation: Security updates are designed to address specific vulnerabilities, effectively closing doors that attackers might exploit.
- Protection against malware: Many malware strains exploit unpatched vulnerabilities to gain access to systems. Applying updates helps prevent malware infections.
- Software performance: Updates can enhance software performance, optimize system resources, and improve user experience.
- Data integrity: Maintaining up-to-date software ensures the integrity of customer and dealership data, preserving trust and reputation.

Challenges and Best Practices

While conducting vulnerability assessments and applying security updates are essential practices, several challenges must be addressed.

- Timeliness: The speed at which vulnerabilities are addressed matters. Delaying security updates can expose the organization to unnecessary risk.
- Resource allocation: Ensuring that dedicated resources are allocated to vulnerability management and patching activities is vital.
- Testing: Before applying security updates to production environments, thorough testing in controlled environments is essential to ensure updates don't inadvertently disrupt operations.
- Vendor collaboration: Keeping track of security bulletins and updates from various software vendors can be complex. Developing a streamlined process for tracking updates is crucial.

Conclusion

Implementing robust network security measures and firewalls is a foundational pillar of cybersecurity for car dealerships. By practicing network segmentation, deploying effective firewalls, utilizing intrusion detection systems, rigorously monitoring logs, conducting regular vulnerability assessments, and promptly applying security updates, dealerships can significantly enhance their defense against cyber threats. These proactive measures shield sensitive information and ensure the uninterrupted operation of dealership services, preserving the trust of customers and stakeholders alike. In an era when cybersecurity threats are ever evolving, establishing a strong network security framework is a proactive step toward maintaining the confidentiality, integrity, and availability of dealership infrastructure and data.

B. SECURE REMOTE ACCESS AND USER AUTHENTICATION PRACTICES

Ensuring secure remote access and robust user authentication practices within car dealerships is akin to safeguarding the entrance to a treasure trove. Just as Ali Baba relied on the phrase "Open Sesame" to protect access to riches, modern dealerships must employ advanced methods to shield valuable data and systems from potential threats.

Virtual Private Networks

Virtual private networks serve as modern gateways to the digital realm, replicating the enchanted phrases of ancient tales. These encrypted tunnels are designed to fortify the pathway between remote devices and dealership networks, ensuring that confidential information remains sheltered despite uncertain digital landscapes.

Two-Factor Authentication

Drawing inspiration from the dual-key mechanism of ancient vaults, two-factor authentication constructs a formidable barricade against unauthorized access. Just as the key and the guard ensured protection, 2FA pairs the familiar password with an additional layer of authentication, reinforcing the digital fortress.

Secure Password Policies

In the annals of history, passwords have long guarded valuable secrets. Today, dealership cyber guardians draw inspiration from this tradition, weaving complex and resilient passwords. Similar to crafting intricate locks for ancient doors, modern password policies set the stage for the first line of defense against cyber invaders.[99]

The Sentinel's Watch: Ensuring Comprehensive Identity and Access Security

The quest for robust identity and access security within car dealerships is akin to guarding a treasure trove's entrance. Just as ancient fortresses required vigilant sentinels to discern friend from foe, modern dealerships must deploy advanced measures to ensure only authorized users can access their digital domain.

Contextual Identity: Unlocking a New Realm of Access

Identification of users requesting access to a system is paramount. Multifactor authentication emerges as the talisman that elevates identification. In contrast to rudimentary password-based systems, multifactor authentication transcends, offering a heightened ability to identify access requests accurately. This enhanced identification leads to personalized access privileges based on context. Adhering to the doctrine of least privilege, users are endowed with only those rights necessary for their roles, ensuring that the security fabric remains robust. This cornerstone of differentiated access aligns seamlessly with modern authorization capabilities, such as those found in Citrix NetScaler.

Bastions of Network Security: A Multilayered Vigil

The burgeoning demand for remote access injects complexity into the guardianship of network security. Nevertheless, the sanctity of network integrity must stand unwavering, even while supporting remote entry points for mobile and third-party voyagers. The network and host segmentation concept emerges as the bulwark against vulnerabilities, effectively shrinking the vulnerable surfaces open to attack. The fortress of network security fortified by a multilayered approach safeguards availability and enhances the sentinels' watch against potential threats.[100]

---

[99] https://citrixready.citrix.com/content/dam/ready/program/secure-remote-access-program/pdf-censornetmfaadvancednetscalerguide-web.pdf.
[100] https://jumpcloud.com/blog/passwordless-authentication-vs-multi-factor-authentication.

Safeguarding the Gates: Fortifications of Application Security

In the sprawling domain of digitized commerce, applications of every nature stand as potential targets for adversaries. However, the surge in application proliferation has expanded the battlefield for nefarious actors. Mobile applications, in particular, present an alluring prize for exploitation. The strategy of centralization and encrypted delivery emerges as the shield against these vulnerabilities, safeguarding the digital gates against infiltrations. The concept of containerization, akin to securing precious cargo, further insulates the data, both in transit and at rest, enhancing the shield against potential breaches.

Data as the Crown Jewel: Fortifying Data Security

The crown jewel of every digital realm is its data. Safeguarding enterprise data requires more than just walls; it necessitates centralization and the sanctuary of hosted delivery. Secure file sharing, akin to granting access to treasured scrolls, curtails data loss, while data containerization, both in motion and at rest, wraps a cloak of invulnerability around this cherished possession.

The Vigil Continues: Monitoring and Swift Response

In this ever-evolving narrative of cybersecurity, vigilance remains paramount. Daily skirmishes against an array of threats demand unwavering watchfulness. Yet even the most fortified fortresses may face successful attacks. Swift response to breaches is the final line of defense against imminent incursions. End-to-end visibility into application traffic is the beacon guiding rapid detection of anomalies and security breaches, minimizing damage, and fortifying against impending onslaughts.

In the Modern Tale of Cybersecurity

As the digital era unfolds, the fable of password protection evolves. The days of "Open Sesame" are recast into multifaceted challenges that guard access to prized digital assets. In this narrative, the dealership leaders are wise sages selecting advanced authentication solutions to fit their needs. They choose from the three options available: one-factor, two-factor, or multifactor authentication. These choices, much like the enchanted keys of lore, unlock the doors to the dealership's virtual kingdom.

In contrast to the ancient tale where children sought access to hidden treasures, modern employees navigate digital realms where treasures are data, customer information, and sensitive systems. With cybersecurity tools, dealerships forge new security legends, thwarting digital thieves and ensuring that only the rightful users gain passage.

Conclusion

In this modern retelling, the dealership's cybersecurity landscape emerges as a realm with opportunities for safeguarding valuable resources. Through VPNs, 2FA, fortified password policies, and vigilant access management, dealerships create their own stories of resilience against cyber adversaries. With these security measures in place, the dealership's digital vaults remain impervious, allowing for seamless remote access while upholding the legacy of protection. Just as ancient tales enthralled generations, the modern tale of cybersecurity underscores the importance of adapting age-old wisdom to guard against contemporary digital threats.

C. NETWORK MONITORING AND INTRUSION DETECTION/PREVENTION SYSTEMS: SAFEGUARDING DEALERSHIP CYBERSECURITY

Maintaining cybersecurity requires more than technological prowess; it demands a proactive approach. Network monitoring and intrusion detection/prevention systems are at the forefront of this approach, powerful tools that play a pivotal role in defending the virtual domain. Let's delve into their multifaceted functions and the advantages they bring to the table.

Role of Network Monitoring: Fortifying Digital Boundaries

In the ever-expanding digital landscape, where data flows like a virtual river, ensuring the integrity of the dealership's cyber boundaries is a formidable challenge. This is where network monitoring steps in as the guardian of the digital gates. Picture it as a vigilant sentry standing watch over the network, meticulously scanning every byte of data entering and exiting. Its role is to oversee network traffic, scrutinize user activities, and monitor system behaviors with hawklike precision.

Network monitoring serves a dual purpose: to detect ongoing attacks and to identify suspicious activities that might indicate an impending threat. Analyzing patterns and anomalies in data traffic acts as the first line of defense, alerting cybersecurity teams to potential security breaches. This proactive stance empowers dealerships to respond swiftly and decisively, minimizing the potential damage inflicted by cyber adversaries.[101]

Benefits of Real-Time Monitoring: Swift and Informed Action

Real-time monitoring is the heartbeat of these systems. It operates around the clock, continuously observing and evaluating digital activities as they unfold. Imagine a virtual auditor that never sleeps, tirelessly analyzing the digital landscape for deviations from the norm. This real-time vigilance guarantees the immediate identification of anomalies or suspicious behaviors.

Consider a scenario where a dealership employee inadvertently clicks on a phishing link, triggering a potential breach. Real-time monitoring swiftly identifies this unusual behavior—the "unknown unknown"—and raises the alarm. Cybersecurity personnel can then spring into action, assessing the situation, isolating affected systems, and neutralizing the threat before it spirals out of control.

Log Analysis

Just as an astute detective sifts through clues to solve a case, log analysis delves into the digital breadcrumbs left behind by users and systems. These logs, akin to the trails left in the digital landscape, hold invaluable insights into the inner workings of the network. They chronicle user interactions, system activities, and network connections.

Intrusion detection/prevention systems decipher patterns and anomalies that might elude human scrutiny. Consider the analogy of a massive jigsaw puzzle. While each log entry might seem insignificant, they form a comprehensive picture of the dealership's digital activities. It enables early detection of potential threats, allowing cybersecurity experts to act proactively and prevent potential breaches from escalating.

---

[101] https://insights.sei.cmu.edu/blog/cybersecurity-architecture-part-2-system-boundary-and-boundary-protection/.

Harnessing Threat Intelligence

In the realm of cybersecurity, knowledge is the ultimate shield. This is where threat intelligence comes into play. Intrusion detection/prevention systems tap into a vast repository of global threat intelligence, drawing on insights from cybersecurity experts, researchers, and collaborative platforms. By integrating this collective wisdom, these systems become fortified against various threats.

Consider a new strain of malware identified halfway across the world. Threat intelligence platforms promptly share information about this threat's characteristics, behaviors, and attack vectors. This data is ingested by intrusion detection/prevention systems, enabling them to recognize the telltale signs of this malware and respond proactively, even before the threat arrives at the dealership's doorstep.

Addressing Threats

Swift and effective incident response is the hallmark of a resilient cybersecurity strategy. When network monitoring and intrusion detection/prevention systems detect suspicious activities or potential threats, they trigger predefined incident response procedures. This orchestrated approach ensures that every potential threat is met with a rapid and coordinated countermeasure.

Imagine a malicious actor attempting to breach the dealership's network. The intrusion detection system identifies this unauthorized access attempt and immediately raises an alert. Incident response teams swing into action, isolating affected systems, blocking malicious traffic, and initiating recovery. This proactive response minimizes the threat's impact and maintains business continuity.

Conclusion

Network monitoring and intrusion detection/prevention systems emerge as steadfast protectors in the intricate dance between cybersecurity and modern dealerships. They wield real-time monitoring, log analysis, threat intelligence integration, and incident response procedures to shield the dealership's digital assets from cyber adversaries. These information-driven tools underscore the symbiosis of technology and vigilance, preserving the integrity of digital operations and ensuring business continuity in the face of evolving cyber challenges. As dealerships navigate the complex digital landscape, network monitoring and intrusion detection/prevention systems stand as the stalwart guardians of their virtual fortresses, keeping cyber threats at bay and allowing the dealership's operations to flourish securely.

CHAPTER 11

APPLICATION SECURITY: SAFEGUARDING DEALERSHIP SOFTWARE AND SYSTEMS

A. BEST PRACTICES FOR SECURE SOFTWARE DEVELOPMENT AND MAINTENANCE

The role of software is pivotal for any car dealership in the contemporary era. However, this reliance on software exposes dealerships to cyber threats that exploit vulnerabilities in their digital ecosystem. Safeguarding dealership software and systems necessitates a comprehensive approach, encompassing secure software development and meticulous maintenance practices. This section delves into these practices, highlighting their pivotal role in upholding a robust cybersecurity defense.

Elevating Security through Coding Practices

A commitment to robust coding practices is at the core of secure software development. These practices establish the foundation upon which secure applications are built. By rigorously adhering to industry-standard coding guidelines, developers can proactively address potential vulnerabilities that cybercriminals frequently exploit. Techniques, such as input validation, output encoding, and parameterized queries, are potent defenses against common threats like injection attacks and cross-site scripting. Secure coding resonates with constructing a fortified structure, setting the groundwork for endurance amid the relentless challenges of the digital domain.[102]

Code Reviews

Code reviews emerge as a cohesive defense mechanism. This collaborative practice involves experienced developers meticulously scrutinizing code to unearth vulnerabilities, logical inconsistencies, and alignment with security benchmarks. Code reviews transcend quality assurance; they function as vigilant sentinels identifying and rectifying latent vulnerabilities before they become severe security breaches. This collective approach fosters an environment of perpetual enhancement while constructing an impenetrable shield against potential threats.

---

[102] https://www.mckinsey.com/~/media/mckinsey/industries/automotive%20and%20assembly/our%20insights/cybersecurity%20in%20automotive%20mastering%20the%20challenge/cybersecurity-in-automotive-mastering-the-challenge.pdf.

Embracing Vulnerability Scanning

In the intricate complexities of software architecture, vulnerabilities often lurk beneath the surface, imperceptible to untrained eyes. Here, vulnerability scanning tools wield their power, systematically traversing the software stack to uncover latent weaknesses. These scans leave no stone unturned, scrutinizing operating systems, third-party libraries, and every component. Car dealerships can proactively detect and address latent vulnerabilities through regular vulnerability assessments, systematically reducing the attack surface and fortifying their digital defenses.

Secure Software Supply Chain Management

Modern software development mirrors the creation of an intricate tapestry, where each component contributes to the larger masterpiece. Yet with each addition, the potential for vulnerabilities to creep in grows. Secure software supply chain management is a vigilant curator ensuring that every third-party component undergoes rigorous security vetting. This practice guards against infiltrating vulnerable or malicious code into the software, shielding the dealership from accidental security breaches.

Cybersecurity Prioritization

Every manager and developer interviewed acknowledged the importance of cybersecurity and its integration into products. Nevertheless, both sides often need to catch up to address this crucial aspect. This discrepancy arises from misconceptions that cybersecurity doesn't directly contribute to revenue and that it can be easily added later in the development process. These misguided notions lead to prioritizing cybersecurity below revenue-generating features, often resulting in late-stage additions after vulnerabilities are uncovered.

Lackluster cybersecurity can negatively impact revenue. While some executives believe customers will pay less for cybersecurity, it's increasingly becoming a priority. Corporate customers thoroughly vet software purchases, explicitly asking for cybersecurity measures and independent security testing. Even for unique market-desirable features, bolstering cybersecurity is becoming a prerequisite.

Cybersecurity Isn't Easy to Add Later

Despite lip service to security, many software development processes don't prioritize security from the outset. Security is often considered only when vulnerabilities emerge, leading to potentially high costs for retroactive fixes. Some leaders prioritize releasing products quickly to meet market demands, even if they are vulnerable. This approach risks leaving customers to manage vulnerabilities in their supply chain.

Cybersecurity as an afterthought can be challenging and costly. Retrofitting cybersecurity into offerings introduces additional expenses, delays, and potential redesigns. Leaders must address these misconceptions directly, ensuring a robust and secure supply chain.

Conclusion

As we navigate the complexities of application security, we unearth strategies to navigate dealerships' evolving challenges. By embracing secure software development practices and unwavering maintenance, dealerships erect a stronghold against the relentless tide of cyber threats. Secure software development and meticulous maintenance are the bedrock of a resilient digital infrastructure where customer data remains inviolate, operations continue unimpeded, and the dealership's reputation remains untarnished.

B. REGULAR SOFTWARE UPDATES AND PATCH MANAGEMENT TO ADDRESS VULNERABILITIES

In the intricate web of dealership software and systems, regular software updates and diligent patch management stand as stalwart guardians against the ever-evolving landscape of cyber threats. The imperatives of cybersecurity demand that car dealerships remain vigilant in securing digital fortresses. This section underscores the importance of staying up to date through consistent software updates and robust patch management practices.

Addressing Vulnerabilities through Vigilant Updates

The digital world is a dynamic realm marked by the constant ebb and flow of innovation and security challenges. In this landscape, software vulnerabilities are akin to chinks in the armor, offering opportunistic cybercriminals a foothold for infiltration. Regular software updates are the digital equivalent of shoring up defenses, fortifying the system against the onslaught of evolving threats. These updates encompass feature enhancements and crucial security patches designed to plug vulnerabilities.

The Benefits of Regular Updates: A Multifaceted Approach

Software updates come bearing a trove of benefits, each aimed at enhancing the functionality and security of digital systems. They bring a realm of revisions, from security hole patching to introducing novel features. These updates serve as a testament to the evolving nature of digital solutions, ensuring that software remains relevant, efficient, and fortified against emerging threats.

Harnessing the Power of Security Patching

In cybersecurity, security flaws and vulnerabilities present a constant challenge. Hackers meticulously seek these chinks in the digital armor to exploit for their nefarious gains. A vulnerability in software, if left unchecked, can become the conduit for cyberattacks. This is where software updates shine as defenders of the digital domain. These updates often come bundled with security patches, as virtual barriers to thwart hackers' advances.[103]

Preserving Your Digital Fortresses

In today's interconnected world, personal data is a prized possession, and cybercriminals are eager to lay their hands on it. Your device contains many personal and sensitive information, from emails to financial records. Inadequately secured software poses a risk to this treasure trove. Cybercriminals can exploit these vulnerabilities to commit identity theft, financial fraud or deploy ransomware attacks. Regular software updates erect a virtual bulwark, safeguarding your data and ensuring your digital sanctuary remains impregnable.

---

[103] https://www.dnsstuff.com/vulnerability-and-patch-management.

It's Not Just about You: The Ripple Effect of Cybersecurity

The consequences of a cybersecurity breach extend beyond an individual. A compromised device can become a vector for spreading malicious software to friends, family, and colleagues. By neglecting software updates, you inadvertently put these connections at risk. The ripple effect of cybersecurity underscores the shared responsibility of maintaining updated software and systems. As you bolster your digital defenses, you contribute to the collective resilience against cyber threats.[104]

Embracing Progress through Updates

Software updates are more than security measures; they represent a constant pursuit of progress. They inject fresh vitality into existing features, rectify issues, and enhance performance. As technology marches forward, software updates empower you to stay in sync with the times. These updates are a declaration of your commitment to embracing the latest and greatest that the digital world has to offer.[105]

The Perils of Outdated Software

Allowing software to stagnate in its current state poses significant risks to dealership cybersecurity. Outdated software becomes a breeding ground for exploits, with attackers targeting known vulnerabilities that lack the protective cover of patches. Cybercriminals thrive on such vulnerabilities, representing low-hanging fruit in their quest for unauthorized access and data breaches. Consequently, the importance of timely updates cannot be overstated as they serve as a bulwark against opportunistic cyber threats.

The Breeding Ground for Exploits

With its static code and stagnant defenses, outdated software becomes a fertile breeding ground for cyber exploits. It's like leaving a gateway open for malicious actors to stroll uninvited. Attackers are adept at pinpointing and exploiting known vulnerabilities no longer shielded by the protective layers of patches and updates. These vulnerabilities, often well-documented

---

[104] https://hbr.org/2021/05/is-third-party-software-leaving-you-vulnerable-to-cyberattacks.
[105] https://us.norton.com/blog/how-to/the-importance-of-general-software-updates-and-patches.

in the cybersecurity community, become prime targets for cybercriminals seeking unauthorized access, data breaches, and potential financial gain.

Weakest Links

For cybercriminals, outdated software vulnerabilities represent a compelling opportunity. They are the low-hanging fruit in the sprawling orchard of potential targets. Just as a seasoned thief might target an unlocked door in a row of secured houses, attackers will gravitate toward the weakest links in a dealership's digital infrastructure. With vulnerabilities that lack the fortified defenses provided by updates, cybercriminals can strike with relative ease, making off with sensitive data or causing operational disruptions.

The Importance of Timely Updates

The pivotal role of timely updates in cybersecurity cannot be overstated. Updates are the vanguard against opportunistic cyber threats, shoring up defenses against potential exploits. By implementing updates promptly, dealerships erect a bulwark of protection around their digital assets, making it considerably harder for attackers to infiltrate systems and compromise sensitive information.

A Multifaceted Defense

Addressing the perils of outdated software involves more than a simple act of updating. It entails orchestrating a multifaceted defense encompassing the technical aspect and cultivating a cybersecurity-conscious culture within the organization.

Technical Vigilance

Technical vigilance involves a proactive stance in identifying and implementing software updates promptly. It's a commitment to staying informed about the latest security patches and fixes software vendors provide. This diligence extends to all layers of the digital ecosystem, from operating systems to applications and frameworks. A well-maintained software ecosystem is the cornerstone of a resilient cybersecurity posture.

Cultivating Cyber Hygiene

Beyond the technical realm, cultivating a culture of cyber hygiene is equally imperative. It entails instilling awareness among employees about the risks posed by outdated software and the crucial role of updates. Regular training sessions and communication initiatives can empower the workforce to identify and report potential vulnerabilities, fostering a collaborative approach to cybersecurity.

Navigating the Update Paradox

It's worth noting that while updates are pivotal for security enhancement, they can occasionally introduce their challenges. Compatibility issues, unexpected system behavior, and potential disruptions must be managed judiciously. A well-structured update management strategy involves thorough testing and evaluation before deployment to ensure that the cure doesn't inadvertently become poison.

Automated Patching

Automated patching processes emerge as a beacon of efficiency, ensuring vulnerabilities are swiftly addressed without delay. These automated mechanisms streamline the deployment of patches, minimizing the window of vulnerability and reducing the burden on IT staff. Dealerships can enhance security and free up valuable resources for other critical tasks by automating patch management.

Strategies for Effective Patch Testing and Deployment

While the significance of prompt updates is undeniable, the deployment process requires cautious steps and meticulous planning. Let's explore the strategies that underpin successful patch testing and deployment.

Thorough Patch Testing

Quickly deploying patches can sometimes lead to unforeseen complications. A comprehensive patch-testing strategy provides a solution. By testing patches in controlled environments, dealerships can anticipate potential issues and conflicts before a full-scale rollout.

Setting Up Controlled Environments

Effective patch deployment is a calculated progression. Controlled environments act as testing grounds, allowing patches to be introduced away from the live infrastructure, which helps to identify unexpected challenges.

Strategic Planning

Strategic planning is key. Dealerships should establish clear road maps outlining testing, validation, and deployment stages. Phased rollout approaches offer safety nets against unforeseen consequences, enabling swift corrective measures.

Ensuring Transparency and Accountability through Documentation

Detailed documentation serves as a record of transparency and accountability. Maintained at every stage, it highlights decision-making processes, technical details, and outcomes, providing valuable insights for future deployments.

The Intersection of Strategy and Execution

The synergy between strategy and execution defines successful patch testing and deployment. Strategy charts the course through uncharted territory, while execution translates plans into tangible actions.

Conclusion

The quest for secure software and systems remains unceasing in a digital landscape brimming with both innovation and peril. Regular software updates and vigilant patch management constitute the backbone of this quest, ensuring that vulnerabilities are addressed promptly and thoroughly. By keeping pace with the ever-changing cybersecurity landscape, dealerships stand poised to thwart the ambitions of cybercriminals and protect their critical assets.

As we delve deeper into safeguarding dealership software and systems, these practices unveil themselves as integral components of a holistic cybersecurity strategy. Embracing regular updates and robust patch management is akin to forging an unyielding armor, ready to repel the advances of cyber threats and preserve the integrity of the digital realm. Through unwavering dedication to these practices, dealerships affirm their commitment to customer trust, operational resilience, and the sustained triumph of cybersecurity in an evolving digital age.

C. IMPLEMENTING SECURE CODING PRACTICES AND CONDUCTING SECURITY ASSESSMENTS

A comprehensive strategy for cybersecurity hinges on two crucial pillars: the systematic implementation of secure coding practices and the rigorous execution of thorough security assessments. These twin endeavors lay the groundwork for an impregnable digital fortress, shielding car dealerships from potential cyber threats with unwavering resolve.

Secure Coding Practices

Any resilient software's core lies a foundation built on secure coding practices. These practices encompass meticulously crafted guidelines and techniques engineered to mitigate vulnerabilities and infuse applications with resilience from their inception. By incorporating these practices into the development fabric, programmers can preemptively guard against a myriad of potential security breaches.

Harnessing Secure Coding Frameworks

Secure coding frameworks constitute a structured approach to creating impervious software. These frameworks provide developers with meticulously curated directives and best practices, forming a cohesive blueprint for handling common vulnerabilities. The result is a harmonized and fortified coding process that forms the bedrock of software security.

Secure Code Reviews

Secure code reviews stand as sentinels of security within the development process. These reviews entail a thorough examination of the code base by seasoned professionals. This meticulous analysis unveils latent vulnerabilities and weak points before they can be exploited by malicious actors, ensuring that the software's integrity remains unblemished.

Secure Coding Training

Knowledge is the sword with which developers fend off vulnerabilities. Secure coding training equips developers with a comprehensive understanding of robust coding techniques. Through these training programs, developers gain insights into common vulnerabilities, security best practices, and coding methodologies that reduce risk exposure.

Periodic Security Assessments

More than static defense is required in the rapidly evolving landscape of cybersecurity threats. Car dealerships must engage in proactive measures to assess and adapt to emerging risks. This involves periodic security assessments that scrutinize the software's resilience, identifying potential vulnerabilities that may have emerged over time.

Static Code Analysis

Static code analysis offers a glimpse into the software's blueprint without its execution. This meticulous examination involves scrutinizing the code base for coding errors, vulnerabilities, and alignment with secure coding standards. This preemptive assessment is a sentinel against vulnerabilities that may attempt to infiltrate the final product.

Penetration Testing

Penetration testing replicates real-world cyberattacks to evaluate the software's resistance to breaches. Ethical hackers, skilled in penetration testing, simulate cyberattacks to identify potential vulnerabilities that malicious actors could exploit. This process serves as a litmus test for the software's resilience under duress.

Synthesis of Digital Resilience

The convergence of secure coding practices and methodical security assessments results in the synthesis of digital resilience. Developers erect fortified defenses from within the software's architecture through secure coding. Simultaneously, security assessments provide a proactive mechanism for threat detection, ensuring that vulnerabilities are exposed and rectified before they can be weaponized.

Conclusion

In the ceaseless battle against cyber threats, the efforts of secure coding practices and meticulous security assessments stand as steadfast guardians. By infusing secure code and subjecting systems to comprehensive scrutiny, car dealerships pave the path to an impervious digital landscape. This commitment to digital fortification ensures that the dealership's software and systems remain unassailable in the face of the ever-evolving challenges presented by modern cyber adversaries.

CHAPTER 12

ENDPOINT SECURITY: SECURING DEALERSHIP DEVICES AND WORKSTATIONS

A. STRATEGIES FOR PROTECTING DEALERSHIP ENDPOINTS AGAINST CYBER THREATS

In the intricate web of modern cybersecurity, endpoint protection stands as a sentinel guarding the entry points to an organization's digital realm. Dealerships, reliant on many devices, such as desktops, laptops, and mobile devices, must weave a robust shield against the relentless onslaught of cyber threats. This section delves into various indispensable strategies for safeguarding dealership endpoints from cyber dangers.

The Vigilance of Endpoint Protection Solutions

A fortified defense starts with the right tools. Endpoint protection solutions form a bulwark against the multifaceted threats looming in the digital landscape. Antivirus software is at the forefront of this defense, a vigilant guardian that identifies and eradicates malware, including viruses, worms, and trojans. By neutralizing malicious code, antivirus software shields sensitive data and prevents disruptive cyber incidents.[106]

Complementing this defense are firewalls, the digital bastions determining the legitimacy of incoming and outgoing network traffic. Firewalls act as sentinels blocking unauthorized access attempts while permitting legitimate communication. To further fortify the defense, intrusion prevention systems (IPS) monitor network traffic in real time, swiftly identifying and thwarting unauthorized access and known attack patterns.

Navigating a Dynamic Landscape

Complacency is a costly luxury. Regular operating systems and security software updates are vital to maintaining a resilient defense. Operating system patches play a crucial role in plugging vulnerabilities exploited by hackers. These patches eliminate security gaps, reducing the potential attack surface for cyber adversaries.[107]

Equally significant are updates to endpoint protection software. As cyber threats evolve, security software must stay attuned to the changing threat landscape. Regular updates ensure the latest threat definitions are

---

[106] https://www.crowdstrike.com/cybersecurity-101/endpoint-security/.

[107] https://cybersecurity.att.com/blogs/security-essentials/endpoint-protection-explained.

integrated, empowering the software to effectively identify and neutralize emerging threats.

Vigilant Vulnerability Management

A proactive approach to cybersecurity necessitates vigilant vulnerability management. This strategy entails identifying, evaluating, and mitigating potential weaknesses in endpoints. Automated tools conduct regular vulnerability assessments, scanning for vulnerabilities ranging from outdated software to misconfigurations.

Upon identification, vulnerabilities are prioritized based on severity. Critical vulnerabilities, if exploited, could lead to catastrophic breaches and must be addressed promptly. This prioritization informs the deployment of patches and updates, ensuring that potential pathways for exploitation are swiftly closed.

Cultivating Cybersecurity Awareness

Technology alone cannot ensure a formidable defense; a well-informed workforce is essential to endpoint security. Dealerships must invest in cybersecurity education and training to empower employees to recognize and respond to threats. Regular training sessions and simulated phishing exercises bolster vigilance, transforming employees into a robust line of defense.[108]

Securing the Mobile Frontier

The proliferation of mobile devices introduces a new dimension of vulnerability. These devices transcend traditional network boundaries, making them susceptible to various threats. Adopting mobile device management (MDM) solutions is imperative to counteract these risks.

MDM solutions grant centralized control over mobile devices, enabling secure configurations, application management, and remote wipe capabilities. Employing strong authentication mechanisms and encrypting mobile devices further enhances the security of sensitive data accessed through these endpoints.

---

[108] https://www.isaca.org/resources/isaca-journal/issues/2019/volume-2/how-to-increase-cybersecurity-awareness.

The Importance of Endpoint Security Measures

These endpoints, including desktops, laptops, and mobile devices, are the entry points to a dealership's digital infrastructure. A comprehensive strategy must encompass deploying robust endpoint protection solutions to counteract the array of cyber threats. This section delves into the paramount importance of these solutions and their components: antivirus software, firewalls, and intrusion prevention systems.[109]

Antivirus

Antivirus software is the digital shield that protects against relentless malware. It is a quintessential component of endpoint security, scanning files and applications for malicious code, viruses, trojans, and other forms of malware. By identifying and neutralizing these threats, antivirus software safeguards sensitive data, prevents unauthorized access, and preserves the integrity of digital operations.

Antivirus software's real-time protection is paramount in a world where malware mutates and evolves astonishingly. It continuously updates its database with the latest threat definitions, enabling it to identify and thwart emerging threats promptly.

Firewalls

Firewalls serve as the virtual gatekeepers of digital communication, regulating data flow between an endpoint and the network. They act as barriers against unauthorized access attempts, monitoring incoming and outgoing network traffic to ensure it adheres to predefined security rules.

Firewalls are particularly effective in preventing unauthorized access, such as cyberattacks attempting to exploit vulnerabilities or gain unauthorized access to sensitive information. By filtering traffic based on predefined rules and policies, firewalls ensure that only legitimate and safe communication is permitted while blocking potentially malicious activity.

---

[109] https://contentsecurity.com.au/managed-cyber-security-awareness-program/.

Intrusion Prevention Systems

Intrusion prevention systems elevate endpoint protection to a proactive level. Unlike firewalls, which primarily focus on blocking unauthorized access, IPS actively monitors network traffic in real time to detect and prevent known attack patterns and suspicious activities.

IPS solutions are adept at identifying anomalies that could indicate cyber threats, such as patterns associated with distributed denial of service attacks or brute-force attempts to gain access. IPS can trigger automated responses upon detection, such as blocking malicious traffic or alerting security personnel for further investigation.

Conclusion

Endpoint protection solutions, encompassing antivirus software, firewalls, and intrusion prevention systems, are the bedrock of modern cybersecurity for dealerships. In a digital landscape teeming with threats, these solutions play a pivotal role in preventing unauthorized access, data breaches, and disruptions to operations.

The Need for Regular Updates

In pursuing a robust cybersecurity posture, implementing strategies for protecting dealership endpoints goes beyond deploying security solutions alone. Addressing the need for regular endpoint security updates and effective vulnerability management is essential to this overarching defense strategy.[110]

The Significance of Regular Endpoint Security Updates

Endpoints are not static entities; they are in a perpetual interaction state with the digital world. As such, they are susceptible to a constantly evolving landscape of cyber threats. Regular endpoint security updates play a pivotal role in maintaining the resilience of these devices in the face of emerging vulnerabilities.

---

[110] https://us.norton.com/blog/how-to/the-importance-of-general-software-updates-and-patches.

Software developers and security experts continually identify and rectify security flaws within software applications and operating systems. Endpoint security updates, or patches, deliver these critical fixes to devices, effectively closing the door on potential exploits. Without these updates, known vulnerabilities remain unaddressed, offering cybercriminals an open invitation to breach endpoints and compromise sensitive data.

Timely security updates are not merely a convenience but a necessity. They are virtual armor shielding devices against known threats, preventing unauthorized access and data breaches. Without regular updates, dealership endpoints become susceptible to exploits that could be easily mitigated with the right security measures.

Vulnerability Assessment

Vulnerability management is the strategic approach to identifying, assessing, and mitigating potential weaknesses within an organization's digital infrastructure. For dealerships, effective vulnerability management is a proactive stance against cyber threats, ensuring that any existing vulnerabilities are promptly addressed before malicious actors can exploit them.[111]

The process begins with regular vulnerability assessments, which involve scanning endpoints and systems for known security flaws. These assessments provide a comprehensive view of potential weaknesses and serve as a foundation for devising a prioritized remediation plan.

A Holistic Approach to Endpoint Security

Protecting dealership endpoints against cyber threats requires a comprehensive strategy beyond initial security measures. Regular endpoint security updates and effective vulnerability management are integral to this strategy, ensuring that devices remain resilient and fortified against evolving threats.

By embracing regular security updates, dealerships demonstrate a commitment to maintaining the integrity of their digital infrastructure. Timely patching closes doors to potential exploits, reducing the attack surface for cybercriminals. Simultaneously, effective vulnerability

---

[111] https://www.fortinet.com/blog/industry-trends/the-need-for-endpoint-security-isnt-going-away.

management empowers dealerships to proactively identify, assess, and mitigate potential weaknesses, ensuring the security posture remains robust over time.

B. ENDPOINT SECURITY SOLUTIONS, INCLUDING ANTIVIRUS SOFTWARE AND DEVICE ENCRYPTION

In the rapidly evolving cybersecurity landscape, dealerships must marshal a comprehensive arsenal of strategies and technologies to fortify their endpoint security. This section delves into the multifaceted realm of endpoint security solutions, illuminating the pivotal roles played by antivirus software, endpoint detection and response (EDR) solutions, device encryption, and the importance of centralized management.

Antivirus Software

Antivirus software is the vanguard of cybersecurity, acting as a formidable shield against a barrage of known malicious software. Employing a combination of signature-based detection and advanced heuristics, antivirus solutions scrutinize files and applications for telltale signs of malware. By promptly identifying and neutralizing known threats, antivirus software precludes the exploitation of known vulnerabilities, safeguarding devices and data from harm.

Endpoint Detection and Response (EDR) Solutions

The evolving tactics of cybercriminals necessitate a more agile approach to endpoint security. EDR solutions offer a proactive defense strategy by employing sophisticated algorithms and behavioral analysis to detect and respond to threats evading conventional security measures. By continuously monitoring device activities and identifying anomalies, EDR solutions empower security teams to detect and thwart advanced threats in real time.

Device Encryption

The dynamic nature of dealership operations mandates data protection at rest, especially in the context of mobile devices. Device encryption emerges as a potent safeguard, rendering data indecipherable to unauthorized actors.

Using complex encryption algorithms, device encryption transforms data into an unreadable format, ensuring that even compromised devices do not leak sensitive information.[112]

Centralized Management

Effective endpoint security hinges on the cohesive orchestration of diverse security measures. Centralized management emerges as a critical element in this orchestration, facilitating the consistent application of security policies and updates across all endpoints. This streamlined approach enables swift deployment of patches, enforcement of security protocols, and immediate responses to emerging threats.[113]

The Role of Regular Endpoint Security Updates

Dealerships must uphold the principle of continuous improvement to ensure the potency of their endpoint security. Regular updates encompassing security patches, software updates, and vulnerability management are essential. These updates fortify defenses against evolving threats and address known vulnerabilities, ensuring that devices remain resilient in the ever-shifting threat landscape.

Conclusion

Endpoint security solutions encompass a spectrum of tools that collectively establish a fortified barrier against cyber threats. Antivirus software, EDR solutions, device encryption, centralized management, regular updates, and vulnerability management converge to create an intricate protection web. In a landscape where threats are dynamic and relentless, the application of these solutions equips dealerships to safeguard their devices and data with a unified defense mechanism.

---

[112] https://support.microsoft.com/en-us/windows/device-encryption-in-windows-ad5dcf4b-dbe0-2331-228f-7925c2a3012d.

[113] https://www.indeed.com/career-advice/career-development/centralized-management.

C. ENFORCING SECURITY POLICIES AND CONTROLLING ACCESS TO SENSITIVE INFORMATION

In the intricate landscape of endpoint security, an essential layer of defense lies in enforcing rigorous security policies and meticulous control over access to sensitive information. This section delves into the critical role played by these measures in safeguarding dealership endpoints. It emphasizes the significance of robust access controls, user authentication, privileged access management, data loss prevention (DLP), and the insights gained from user behavior analytics.

Robust Access Controls

The digital perimeter of dealership endpoints must be fortified through meticulous access controls. These controls delineate who can access specific resources, applications, and data. By limiting access to authorized personnel only, dealerships thwart unauthorized incursions and fortify their overall security posture.

User Authentication

User authentication serves as the gateway to secure access. Strong authentication mechanisms such as multifactor authentication demand multiple verification forms, drastically reducing the risk of unauthorized access even with compromised credentials. This pivotal measure ensures that only legitimate users gain entry to sensitive information.

Privileged Access Management

Privileged access holds immense power and potential risk. Effective privileged access management (PAM) strategies impose strict controls on high-level permissions. Dealerships should meticulously curate and monitor individuals with privileged access, mitigating the potential for unauthorized use and ensuring accountability.

Data Loss Prevention

The safeguarding of sensitive information is of paramount importance. DLP measures act as sentinels, detecting and preventing unauthorized transmission of sensitive data within and outside the organization. By monitoring data movements and applying content-based rules, DLP solutions ensure that sensitive information remains within authorized boundaries.

User Behavior Analytics

The behaviors and activities of users often harbor critical insights into potential threats. User behavior analytics leverages advanced algorithms to scrutinize user actions, identifying anomalies and deviations from established norms. This approach enables early detection of unauthorized activities, potentially thwarting breaches before they occur.

The Importance of Employee Training and Awareness Regarding Physical Security Threats

A comprehensive security strategy encompasses the virtual world and the physical environment in which dealerships operate. Acknowledging the potential impact of physical security threats, dealerships must prioritize employee training and awareness to create a well-rounded defense against a wide spectrum of risks.

Understanding Physical Security Threats

Physical security threats encompass a range of hazards that can jeopardize a dealership's assets, personnel, and operations. These threats extend beyond the conventional notion of break-ins and burglaries to include various scenarios, such as unauthorized access to sensitive areas, theft of physical documents, sabotage, and even acts of violence. While the digital landscape has gained prominence, physical security threats remain a tangible concern that must be addressed.[114]

Employee Training

A strong defense against physical security threats begins with informed and trained employees. Employees should be educated about potential

---

[114] https://www.deloitte.com/global/en/services/risk-advisory/blogs/physical-security-the-shift-in-perspective.html.

vulnerabilities within the dealership's physical infrastructure, including entrances, exits, storage areas, and sensitive zones. Training sessions should cover aspects like identifying and reporting suspicious activities, understanding emergency protocols, and adhering to access control measures.[115]

Awareness of Social Engineering Tactics

Social engineering tactics often amplify physical security threats that exploit human psychology to gain unauthorized access. Employees should be aware of common tactics like tailgating (when an unauthorized person follows an authorized individual into a secure area), impersonation, and pretexting (creating fabricated scenarios to manipulate individuals into divulging information or granting access). Recognizing these tactics is critical for thwarting attempted breaches.

Securing Physical Assets and Devices

Beyond securing digital assets, dealerships must also secure physical assets like laptops, tablets, and smartphones. Employees should be educated on the importance of physically safeguarding these devices to prevent theft or unauthorized use. This includes guidance on locking devices when not in use, avoiding leaving them unattended in public spaces, and using secure storage solutions.

Emergency Preparedness and Response

Physical security threats can escalate into emergencies that require a swift and coordinated response. Employees should receive training on emergency protocols, evacuation procedures, and communicating effectively during crises. Conducting regular drills ensures that employees are well-prepared to respond to various scenarios, from fire emergencies to natural disasters.

Collaborative Efforts with Security Personnel

Dealerships often employ security personnel who play a crucial role in maintaining physical security. Employee training should emphasize the

---

[115] https://www.rapid7.com/fundamentals/security-awareness-training/.

importance of collaborating with security personnel, reporting suspicious activities promptly, and adhering to their instructions during security incidents. This synergy creates a cohesive defense strategy that maximizes the effectiveness of physical security measures.

Integrating Physical and Cybersecurity Awareness

The lines between physical and cybersecurity are becoming increasingly blurred in the modern interconnected world. Employees should understand how physical actions can have digital consequences and vice versa. For instance, exposing sensitive physical documents in a public area could lead to data breaches if those documents contain sensitive information that can be used for digital attacks.

Conclusion

Implementing stringent security policies and meticulously controlling access to sensitive information from an orchestrated defense against cyber threats. Dealerships construct an intricate and resilient security fabric by employing robust access controls, user authentication, privileged access management, data loss prevention measures, and user behavior analytics. This fabric prevents unauthorized access and provides the insights required to detect and neutralize emerging threats. As the digital landscape evolves, these measures are pillars of protection, ensuring the integrity, confidentiality, and availability of sensitive information on dealership endpoints.

CHAPTER 13

SECURE PAYMENT PROCESSING: PROTECTING CUSTOMER FINANCIAL DATA

A. PAYMENT CARD INDUSTRY (PCI) COMPLIANCE FOR DEALERSHIP PAYMENT PROCESSING

Secure payment processing is an operational necessity and a matter of trust and reputation. As dealerships engage in monetary transactions with customers, protecting sensitive financial data is paramount. This section delves into the crucial concept of Payment Card Industry Data Security Standard (PCI DSS) compliance, providing dealerships with the insights they need to safeguard customer financial information effectively.

Understanding PCI DSS Compliance

The Payment Card Industry Data Security Standard is a set of comprehensive security standards designed to ensure the secure handling of payment card data. These standards apply to organizations that handle credit card information, including car dealerships. Compliance with PCI DSS is a regulatory requirement and a testament to a dealership's commitment to safeguarding customer financial data.[116]

1. Secure Handling of Credit Card Information

PCI DSS compliance places significant emphasis on securing credit card information. Dealerships should implement robust measures to prevent unauthorized access to cardholder data. This involves strict access controls, limiting access to individuals with a legitimate need for such data. Additionally, sensitive data should never be stored unless necessary, and any stored data must be encrypted to thwart potential breaches.

2. Data Encryption and Tokenization

Encryption is a cornerstone of PCI DSS compliance. Encryption ensures that even if data is intercepted, it remains indecipherable to unauthorized parties. Dealerships should implement end-to-end encryption protocols to protect data during transmission. Tokenization is another effective technique wherein sensitive data is replaced with unique tokens, rendering the original data useless to potential attackers.[117]

---

[116] https://files.consumerfinance.gov/f/documents/201908_cfpb_automobile-finance-examination-procedures.pdf.

[117] https://www.pcisecuritystandards.org/.

3. Periodic Vulnerability Assessments

PCI DSS compliance requires regular vulnerability assessments to identify potential weaknesses in systems and processes. Dealerships should conduct comprehensive assessments regularly to proactively identify and address vulnerabilities that could compromise payment card data. These assessments provide valuable insights into the effectiveness of security controls and allow for timely remediation.

4. Penetration Testing

Penetration testing, often called ethical hacking, is a practice to simulate real-world cyberattacks on systems. By conducting controlled attacks, dealerships can uncover vulnerabilities and weaknesses that might otherwise remain hidden. Penetration testing identifies vulnerabilities and allows organizations to gauge their incident response capabilities and enhance their cybersecurity.

5. Building a Culture of Compliance

PCI DSS compliance is not a one-time endeavor; it requires ongoing dedication and adherence to evolving standards. Building a culture of compliance involves educating employees about the importance of secure payment processing, the risks associated with mishandling payment data, and the role each individual plays in maintaining PCI DSS compliance.

6. Integrating Compliance with Customer Trust

Beyond regulatory mandates, PCI DSS compliance is a critical component of maintaining customer trust. Customers entrust dealerships with their financial information, and compliance demonstrates a commitment to protecting that trust. Displaying compliance logos and certifications prominently can reassure customers that their payment information is handled with the utmost care.

Conclusion

Securing customer financial data during payment processing is a nonnegotiable imperative. Dealerships must meet regulatory standards and prioritize the security and integrity of payment transactions. By adhering to PCI DSS compliance requirements, implementing robust encryption and tokenization, conducting regular vulnerability assessments, and fostering a culture of compliance, dealerships can establish a secure payment ecosystem that safeguards customer financial data and fosters unwavering customer trust.

B. SECURE PAYMENT PROCESSING SYSTEMS AND SECURE ONLINE TRANSACTIONS

During the operations of modern businesses, where transactions increasingly occur in the digital realm, ensuring the security of payment processing systems and online transactions is paramount. This section delves into the essential components of creating a secure environment for protecting customer financial data within dealerships.

Secure Payment Processing Systems

Point-to-Point Encryption

Point-to-point encryption (P2PE) is a fortified defense against potential threats within payment processing systems. This technology encrypts sensitive payment card data from the moment it is entered into the system until it reaches its destination. By rendering the data indecipherable to any malicious interceptors, P2PE safeguards customer financial information against unauthorized access.[118]

Secure Payment Gateways

Secure payment gateways are sentinels between the dealership's systems and external payment processors. These gateways encrypt transactional data during its journey, ensuring the information remains incomprehensible even if intercepted. By implementing secure payment gateways, dealerships create a barrier that obstructs any attempts to compromise payment data in transit.

---

[118] https://www.regpacks.com/blog/secure-payment-processing/.

Fraud Detection Mechanisms

Fraud detection mechanisms bring an extra layer of vigilance to payment processing. These systems employ advanced algorithms to scrutinize transaction patterns, promptly identifying irregularities that might suggest fraudulent activities. By acting as a vigilant guardian, fraud detection mechanisms prevent illicit transactions from being processed, thereby shielding customers from potential financial losses.

Strategies for Securing Online Transactions

Secure Sockets Layer Certificates

The bedrock of secure online transactions is the use of secure sockets layer (SSL) certificates. These certificates establish encrypted connections between users' browsers and the dealership's web site. As data is transmitted during online transactions, SSL encryption prevents unauthorized entities from deciphering the information. By integrating SSL certificates, dealerships ensure customer data remains confidential and tamper-proof.

Secure E-commerce Platforms

Selecting a secure e-commerce platform is akin to fortifying the foundation of a secure online transaction environment. Reputable e-commerce platforms have various built-in security features, encompassing secure payment gateways, data encryption, and robust authentication mechanisms. These platforms adhere to industry security standards, providing a fortified platform for online transactions.

Strategies for Secure Online Transactions

Multifactor Authentication

Implementing Multifactor Authentication introduces an additional layer of defense to online transactions. MFA thwarts unauthorized access attempts by mandating users to provide multiple forms of authentication, such as passwords and one-time codes sent to their mobile devices. This mechanism significantly reduces the risk of unauthorized transactions.[119]

---

[119] https://www.loginradius.com/blog/identity/benefits-of-mfa/.

Regular Security Audits

Regular security audits are a proactive approach to maintaining the integrity of online payment systems. These audits systematically evaluate the system's vulnerabilities and strengths, enabling dealerships to identify and address potential weaknesses before exploiting them. Regular audits exhibit a commitment to robust security measures and bolster customer confidence in the dealership's transactional environment.[120]

Conclusion

As the digital landscape evolves, safeguarding customer financial data remains imperative for dealerships. By embracing technologies like point-to-point encryption, secure payment gateways, and fraud detection mechanisms, and by implementing strategies, such as SSL certificates and secure e-commerce platforms, dealerships build a fortress of security around their payment processing systems. These measures protect sensitive customer information and cultivate trust and reliability, solidifying the dealership's reputation as a secure destination for seamless and secure online transactions.

C. SECURE DATA STORAGE AND RETENTION POLICIES FOR FINANCIAL DATA

The responsible storage and retention of customer financial data is a paramount concern for car dealerships. This section delves into the crucial strategies and practices that dealerships can adopt to ensure the secure storage and proper retention of sensitive financial information.

Implementing Secure Data Storage Practices

Data Encryption

The cornerstone of secure data storage is encryption. Employing strong encryption algorithms transforms sensitive financial data into a virtually impossible format for unauthorized parties to decipher. By encrypting data at rest, dealerships ensure that even if physical storage devices are compromised, the information remains incomprehensible and inaccessible.

---

[120] https://www.condorsecurity.ca/6-benefits-getting-security-audit/.

Access Controls

Access controls play a pivotal role in data security. By employing granular access controls, dealerships restrict data access to authorized personnel only. This prevents unauthorized individuals from viewing, modifying, or tampering with sensitive financial information. Strong authentication mechanisms such as multifactor authentication further fortify data access security.

Secure Backup Procedures

Robust backup procedures are essential for safeguarding against data loss due to hardware failures, cyberattacks, or other unforeseen events. Regularly scheduled backups, ideally stored in separate physical locations, ensure that financial data remains intact and recoverable. Backup data should also be encrypted to prevent unauthorized access to sensitive information.

Retention Policies and Compliance

Data Retention Policies

Car dealerships should establish clear and comprehensive data retention policies. These policies dictate how long customer financial data should be stored and under what circumstances it should be securely disposed of. Striking a balance between retaining data for business needs and respecting customer privacy is crucial.

Compliance with Data Protection Regulations

Dealerships dealing with customer financial data are subject to stringent regulations. The Payment Card Industry Data Security Standard and the Gramm-Leach-Bliley Act are two key regulations that govern the handling and protection of financial data. Adhering to these regulations not only ensures legal compliance but also underscores the dealership's commitment to safeguarding customer information.[121]

Data De-Identification and Anonymization

An effective strategy to enhance data security is to de-identify or anonymize stored customer financial data whenever possible. By removing

---

[121] https://www.csoonline.com/article/570281/csos-ultimate-guide-to-security-and-privacy-laws-regulations-and-compliance.html.

personally identifiable information, such as names and credit card numbers, data becomes less attractive to potential attackers. This approach minimizes the impact of a data breach and reduces the risk of identity theft.

Periodic Audits and Continuous Improvement

Regular Data Audits

Periodic data audits ensure data storage and retention practices align with established policies and regulations. These audits evaluate the effectiveness of encryption, access controls, and retention procedures. Any discrepancies or vulnerabilities discovered during audits can be swiftly addressed to maintain a high level of security.

Continuous Employee Training

Human error is a significant factor in data security breaches. Regular and comprehensive employee training programs ensure personnel understand the importance of secure data storage and retention. By keeping employees well-informed about best practices, dealerships create a data security awareness culture.

Conclusion

Safeguarding customer financial data through secure storage and proper retention practices is a legal and ethical obligation and a critical component of building and maintaining customer trust. Car dealerships can ensure that customer financial data remains confidential and protected by implementing robust encryption, access controls, and backup procedures, adhering to data protection regulations, and conducting regular audits. These efforts foster a reputation of reliability, security, and responsible data management, ultimately enhancing the dealership's credibility and customer relationships.

D. COMPLIANCE WITH FINANCIAL REGULATIONS: FAIR CREDIT REPORTING ACT AND RELATED REGULATIONS

The Fair Credit Reporting Act has a significant place in the intricate web of financial regulations governing customer data handling. This section delves into the essence of FCRA and its profound implications for car dealerships when dealing with consumer credit information.

Understanding the Fair Credit Reporting Act

The Fair Credit Reporting Act, enacted by the United States government, is designed to ensure consumer credit information's accuracy, fairness, and privacy. The FCRA primarily applies to the activities of consumer reporting agencies, those who provide credit reports, and those who use these reports to make credit-related decisions. While the FCRA focuses on consumer reporting agencies, car dealerships also fall under its purview when they utilize consumer credit information to facilitate transactions.[122]

Implications for Dealerships

When car dealerships utilize consumer credit information to evaluate creditworthiness and make financing decisions, they become subject to the FCRA's guidelines. Here are the key aspects that dealerships need to consider to ensure compliance:

1. Obtaining Consumer Consent

Dealerships must obtain consumer consent before accessing their credit reports. This consent is a pivotal requirement and is often obtained through the completion of credit application forms. Clear and transparent communication regarding the purpose of credit checks and the potential impact on credit scores is essential to ensure informed consent.

2. Using and Disclosing Consumer Credit Information

Under the FCRA, dealerships should have a permissible purpose for accessing consumer credit reports. Everyday purposes include facilitating vehicle financing or leasing transactions. It's essential to ensure that consumer credit information is only used for legitimate and authorized purposes.

3. Ensuring Accuracy and Privacy

Dealerships must take steps to ensure the accuracy of consumer credit information. This includes verifying the authenticity of the information

---

[122] https://www.bing.com/search?q=Business+System+Vulnerabilities+automotive+industry&qs=ds&form=CONVAJ&showconv=1#.

provided and promptly addressing any discrepancies. Additionally, the FCRA mandates consumer privacy protection, restricting the sharing of credit information without a valid reason.[123]

4. Compliance with FTC and Related Financial Regulations

The Federal Trade Commission oversees and enforces the FCRA to ensure compliance. Noncompliance with FCRA regulations can result in severe penalties and legal actions. In addition to FCRA, car dealerships should also be aware of other related financial regulations, such as the following:

- Truth in Lending Act: This regulation emphasizes transparent communication of loan terms to consumers, ensuring they clearly understand the terms and conditions associated with the credit they obtain.
- Gramm-Leach-Bliley Act: Addressing the privacy and security of customer financial information, GLBA requires dealerships to establish safeguards for protecting nonpublic personal information.
- Antimoney laundering regulations: Car dealerships must also comply with antimoney laundering regulations when engaging in transactions, particularly when large sums of money are involved. This includes verifying the identity of customers to prevent illicit activities.

Conclusion

Compliance with the Fair Credit Reporting Act and related financial regulations is a legal and ethical obligation. Car dealerships play a crucial role in ensuring accuracy, fairness, and privacy of consumer credit information. By obtaining proper consumer consent, using and disclosing credit information for legitimate purposes, and adhering to the guidelines set forth by the FCRA and related regulations, dealerships can protect consumer rights, maintain trust, and uphold the integrity of financial transactions. This commitment to compliance contributes to the dealership's reputation for responsible and ethical business practices in payment processing and consumer credit information handling.

---

[123] https://www.ftc.gov/legal-library/browse/statutes/fair-credit-reporting-act.

CHAPTER 14

INCIDENT DETECTION AND RESPONSE: DETECTING AND RESPONDING TO CYBERTHREATS

A. LEVERAGING SECURITY INFORMATION AND EVENT MANAGEMENT SYSTEMS

In the dynamic and constantly evolving landscape of cybersecurity threats, proactive detection and swift response are paramount. This section delves into the critical role that security information and event management (SIEM) systems play in the context of automotive dealerships, focusing on their significance, components, and incident response capabilities.

Understanding SIEM Systems

At its core, a security information and event management system is a comprehensive platform that offers real-time monitoring, correlation of security events, and incident response capabilities. These systems are designed to collect and analyze data from various sources within the dealership's IT infrastructure, such as network devices, servers, applications, and endpoints. By aggregating this data, SIEM systems provide a holistic view of the dealership's digital environment, enabling the identification of potential threats and vulnerabilities.[124]

The Role of SIEM in Detecting Cyber Threats

SIEM systems function as vigilant sentinels that tirelessly monitor the digital realm for signs of unauthorized or suspicious activities. By analyzing and cross-referencing many data points, SIEM systems can detect patterns and anomalies that might indicate emerging cyber threats. This proactive approach allows dealerships to detect potential breaches in their nascent stages, preventing them from escalating into more serious security incidents.[125]

Critical Components of SIEM Systems

A robust SIEM system consists of several integral components, each contributing to its effectiveness, including the following:

---

[124] https://www.ibm.com/topics/siem.
[125] https://www.fortinet.com/resources/cyberglossary/what-is-siem.

- Data collection: SIEM systems aggregate data from diverse sources, including log files, network traffic, and user behavior, creating a comprehensive dataset for analysis.
- Log correlation: The correlation engine of a SIEM system is responsible for identifying relationships and patterns within the collected data. This ability to connect seemingly disparate events is crucial for recognizing sophisticated cyberattacks.
- Real-time monitoring: SIEM systems continuously monitor events in real time, allowing for immediate detection of anomalies or unusual activities.
- Alerting and notification: When potentially harmful events are identified, SIEM systems generate alerts and notifications for security personnel to take action promptly.

Incident Response Procedures with SIEM Alerts

The power of a SIEM system goes beyond detection; it extends into the realm of incident response.[126] When a SIEM system generates alerts, dealerships can initiate a structured incident response plan.

1. Alert triage: Security professionals analyze the alerts, categorizing them based on urgency and relevance.
2. Investigation: In-depth analysis is conducted to understand the nature and scope of the incident. This involves examining relevant logs, identifying affected systems, and assessing potential impact.
3. Containment: If the incident is confirmed, immediate measures are taken to contain it and prevent further damage.
4. Eradication: The incident's root cause is identified and eradicated to neutralize the threat.
5. Recovery: Affected systems are restored to their normal state, and data integrity is verified.
6. Lessons learned: A comprehensive post-incident analysis is performed to glean insights into vulnerabilities exploited and the efficacy of the response. This information informs future prevention strategies.

---

[126] https://www.exabeam.com/explainers/siem/incident-response-and-automation/.

Conclusion

In the ongoing battle against cyber threats, security information and event management systems stand as stalwart defenders of dealership data. By aggregating and analyzing data, detecting anomalies, and generating alerts, SIEM systems equip dealerships with the tools to proactively identify and respond to potential threats. Furthermore, their role in guiding incident response elevates cybersecurity from a reactive practice to a strategic, dynamic endeavor. By embracing SIEM systems and harnessing their capabilities, dealerships can navigate the intricate cybersecurity landscape with resilience and confidence, safeguarding sensitive information and ensuring the trust of their customers.

B. MASTERING INCIDENT DETECTION TECHNIQUES AND INTRUSION DETECTION/PREVENTION SYSTEMS

Dealerships must use sophisticated tools and techniques to detect and thwart potential security breaches. This section delves into the array of available incident detection techniques and the crucial role of intrusion detection and prevention systems (IDS/IPS) in fortifying the cybersecurity posture of automotive dealerships.

Incident Detection Techniques: Unveiling the Arsenal

Dealerships must adopt a multifaceted approach to incident detection, employing techniques that collectively enhance their ability to detect a diverse range of cyber threats:

- Anomaly detection: This technique establishes a "normal" behavior baseline within the digital environment. Deviations from this baseline, such as unusual network traffic patterns or irregular user activity, trigger alerts for further investigation.
- Signature-based detection: Signature-based detection relies on known malicious code or behavior patterns. It compares network traffic, files, and software against a database of pre-identified signatures associated with known threats.
- Behavior analysis: This technique involves observing user and system behavior to identify deviations from established norms. It often involves the application of machine learning algorithms to

detect subtle anomalies that might escape traditional rule-based systems.[127]

Intrusion Detection/Prevention Systems: Safeguarding Dealership Defenses

IDS/IPS serves as vigilant gatekeepers continuously monitoring network traffic, system logs, and digital interactions to identify signs of unauthorized or malicious activities. These systems play a dual role in detecting and preventing cyber threats:

- Intrusion detection: IDS monitors network traffic and system logs, searching for suspicious patterns that indicate potential threats. When identified, IDS generates alerts that trigger incident response actions.
- Intrusion prevention: Building on IDS, IPS goes further by actively blocking and preventing identified threats from reaching their targets. It employs predefined rules to take immediate action against detected malicious activities.

Incident Response Procedures with IDS/IPS Alerts

When IDS/IPS systems generate alerts, dealerships can initiate a systematic and effective incident response plan.

- Alert prioritization: Security personnel evaluate alerts based on severity and potential impact, prioritizing responses to address the most critical threats.
- Alert investigation: A thorough analysis is conducted to understand the nature and scope of the detected incident. This phase involves examining relevant logs, identifying affected systems, and assessing the potential implications.
- Containment and eradication: If an incident is confirmed, immediate containment measures are taken to prevent further spread. The root cause of the intrusion is identified, and steps are taken to eliminate it.

---

[127] https://ieeexplore.ieee.org/document/7904776.

- Recovery and learning: Affected systems are restored to normal operation, and post-incident analysis is performed to understand the vulnerabilities exploited. These insights inform future security enhancements.

Conclusion

Intrusion detection and prevention systems and a spectrum of incident detection techniques arm dealerships with formidable tools to identify and thwart cyber threats. By leveraging anomaly detection, signature-based detection, and behavior analysis, dealerships can enhance their ability to detect a wide array of malicious activities. Pairing these techniques with the proactive defenses offered by IDS/IPS systems further solidifies cybersecurity defenses. Through meticulous incident response procedures rooted in these alerts, dealerships can dexterously navigate cyber threats, safeguarding customer trust and invaluable data assets.

C. ORCHESTRATING INCIDENT RESPONSE TEAM ROLES AND RESPONSIBILITIES

In the dynamic landscape of modern cybersecurity, the ability to effectively respond to incidents is pivotal. Dealerships must establish a robust incident response team with clear roles and responsibilities. This section delineates the pivotal functions of the incident response team, illuminating the significance of each role in ensuring swift and efficient incident management.

Roles and Responsibilities

- Incident response coordinator: At the helm of the response team, the coordinator oversees the incident management process. This role involves promptly assessing alerts, assigning tasks to team members, and ensuring a seamless flow of communication. The coordinator's steady guidance is instrumental in orchestrating a cohesive response.
- Incident triage specialist: This specialist rapidly assesses the nature and severity of an incident, determining its potential impact. Their

swift decision-making guides the team's initial actions, including escalation to more specialized members if necessary.

- Containment expert: Once an incident is confirmed, the containment expert isolates affected systems. Their actions aim to halt the spread of the threat and prevent further damage.
- Forensic investigator: This expert delves into the heart of the incident, conducting a thorough analysis to uncover the root cause, tactics, techniques, and procedures used by the threat actor. Their insights are pivotal in understanding the scope of the breach.
- Recovery specialist: After containment, the recovery specialist leads the restoration of affected systems to their normal operational state. This role demands meticulous attention to detail to ensure recovery measures do not inadvertently exacerbate the situation.
- Legal and compliance liaison: In today's regulatory landscape, legal and compliance considerations are paramount. This role ensures that the incident response aligns with legal obligations and regulatory requirements, safeguarding the dealership's reputation and legal standing.

Navigating Incident Response Phases: A Choreography of Excellence

- Incident triage: The initial phase involves prompt assessment of the incident's scope, severity, and potential impact. The triage specialist's role comes to the forefront as they swiftly decide to escalate the incident.
- Containment: The containment phase isolates the threat to prevent further harm. The containment expert leads this phase, employing their technical prowess to curtail the threat's reach.
- Investigation: The forensic investigator dives deep into the incident, meticulously reconstructing the sequence of events. Their insights provide a comprehensive understanding of the breach's origin and mechanics.
- Recovery: The recovery specialist takes charge, meticulously restoring affected systems to normal functionality. This phase requires a delicate balance between speed and precision.

- Documentation and analysis: Every action taken during an incident must be documented exhaustively. This documentation provides crucial insights for post-incident analysis and future improvements.
- Lessons learned: Post-incident analysis involves a critical assessment of the incident response process. Lessons learned contribute to refining incident response procedures and fortifying defenses against future threats.

Conclusion

In the intricate dance of incident response, each role in the ensemble plays a pivotal part. The incident response team's coordinated efforts—from swift triage to forensic investigation and from containment to recovery—form a symphony of expertise that thwarts cyber threats. This orchestrated response is not just about resolving the immediate incident; it's about cultivating resilience, learning from challenges, and emerging stronger in the face of evolving cyber threats. The incident response team's dedication and precision are a testament to the dealership's commitment to cybersecurity and customer trust.

CHAPTER 15

SECURITY AUDITS AND ASSESSMENTS: EVALUATING DEALERSHIP CYBERSECURITY

A. CONDUCTING COMPREHENSIVE SECURITY AUDITS AND RISK ASSESSMENTS

Dealerships face an ever-evolving array of threats that can compromise sensitive customer data, disrupt operations, and tarnish reputation. As such, conducting comprehensive security audits and risk assessments has emerged as a paramount practice to evaluate and fortify the robustness of dealership cybersecurity measures. These proactive evaluations provide invaluable insights into potential vulnerabilities, help prioritize security investments, and ensure compliance with industry standards.

Importance of Conducting Comprehensive Security Audits

Comprehensive security audits are a pivotal cornerstone within the cybersecurity framework of modern car dealerships. In an increasingly interconnected digital landscape, where the potential for cyber threats looms large, the significance of these audits cannot be overstated. They represent a crucial line of defense against the ever-evolving tactics of malicious actors seeking to exploit vulnerabilities.[128]

A Holistic Approach to Vulnerability Detection

Unlike ad hoc security measures that may target specific aspects of an organization's digital infrastructure, comprehensive security audits take a panoramic approach. They delve into every nook and cranny of the dealership's technological and procedural landscape. This encompassing methodology ensures that potential weaknesses are brought to light regardless of origin. Audits leave no stone unturned, from the dealership's network infrastructure to its data handling processes. By undertaking a thorough examination, audits can uncover vulnerabilities that might otherwise escape detection in a fragmented security approach.

Proactive Threat Mitigation

In the realm of cybersecurity, prevention is unequivocally better than cure. Comprehensive security audits embody this principle by identifying vulnerabilities before malicious actors exploit them. By proactively

---

[128] https://airiam.com/auto-dealerships-cybersecurity/.

addressing potential weak points, dealerships can thwart cyber threats before they can manifest. This proactive stance significantly reduces the risk of data breaches, unauthorized access, and other cyber incidents that could cripple operations and damage the dealership's reputation.

Empowerment through Knowledge

Comprehensive security audits provide dealerships with a wealth of knowledge about their cybersecurity landscape. The insights gained from these audits empower decision-makers and security professionals to make informed choices. They clearly understand the dealership's strengths, weaknesses, and areas that require immediate attention. With this knowledge, dealerships can allocate resources effectively, implement targeted security measures, and prioritize risk-based vulnerabilities. This strategic empowerment ensures that cybersecurity efforts are focused and impactful.[129]

Staying Ahead of Evolving Threats

The cyber threat landscape is dynamic and adaptive with new attack vectors emerging regularly. Comprehensive security audits are crucial in helping dealerships stay one step ahead of these evolving threats. By continuously assessing their security posture, dealerships can adapt their defenses to counteract new tactics and vulnerabilities. This ongoing vigilance prevents complacency and ensures that the dealership's cybersecurity measures remain relevant and effective.

Enhancing Regulatory Compliance

In an era of stringent data protection regulations, compliance is not an option but a necessity. Comprehensive security audits ensure that dealerships meet regulatory requirements and standards. By identifying gaps in compliance early on, dealerships can take corrective actions to align with industry-specific regulations, such as the Payment Card Industry Data Security Standard and other data protection laws. This safeguards

---

[129] https://www.fisherphillips.com/en/news-insights/auto-dealership-compliance-new-information-security-rules.html.

the organization from legal penalties and demonstrates a commitment to data security and customer privacy.

Fostering Trust and Confidence

The impact of a data breach or cyber incident extends beyond financial losses. It erodes customer trust, damages the dealership's reputation, and undermines stakeholder confidence. Comprehensive security audits directly contribute to building and maintaining trust. By demonstrating a proactive approach to cybersecurity, dealerships are committed to safeguarding customer data and sensitive information. This fosters trust among customers, partners, and stakeholders, solidifying the dealership's standing in the market.

Addressing the Components of a Thorough Security Audit

Within cybersecurity, the complexity and diversity of potential threats dealerships face require a comprehensive approach to security audits. Such audits consist of meticulously planned processes to identify vulnerabilities and weaknesses across the organization's digital landscape.[130] Three pivotal components define a thorough security audit.

1. Network infrastructure review: The foundation of any digital operation lies within its network infrastructure. A comprehensive security audit delves into the intricate architecture of the dealership's network. It includes scrutinizing the configuration of firewalls, routers, switches, and other network devices. The goal is to ensure that access controls are meticulously defined, potential entry points for cyberattackers are minimized, and data flows are securely segmented.
2. Vulnerability scanning: In an ever-evolving cyber threat landscape, staying vigilant against known vulnerabilities is paramount. Vulnerability scanning forms a core element of a thorough security audit. Utilizing specialized software, dealerships systematically scan their systems, applications, and databases to pinpoint known

---

[130] https://www.isaca.org/resources/news-and-trends/industry-news/2022/an-integrated-approach-to-security-audits.

vulnerabilities. This proactive approach enables timely patching and the mitigation of potential risks before they can be exploited.[131]

3. Penetration testing: While vulnerability scanning identifies known weak points, penetration testing further evaluates. Ethical hackers, or penetration testers, simulate actual cyberattacks to assess the robustness of the dealership's defenses. By attempting to breach security measures, they uncover vulnerabilities that automated scans might overlook. This immersive testing enables a deep understanding of potential weaknesses and provides actionable insights for enhancing cybersecurity.

Outlining the Benefits of Risk Assessments

Risk assessments emerge as a strategic linchpin in dealership cybersecurity. By systematically evaluating potential threats, these assessments enable dealerships to identify, quantify, and prioritize vulnerabilities. Two key benefits underscore the significance of risk assessments.

- Identifying vulnerabilities: Risk assessments provide a structured framework to assess vulnerabilities comprehensively. By analyzing the potential impact and likelihood of various cyber risks, dealerships gain insights into the vulnerabilities that pose the greatest threats. This understanding is crucial for focusing mitigation efforts on the most critical areas.

- Prioritizing mitigation efforts: In the face of limited resources, prioritization is crucial. Risk assessments facilitate this process by assigning a risk score to vulnerabilities. This score reflects both the potential impact and likelihood of exploitation. With this information, dealerships can allocate resources strategically, addressing the vulnerabilities that carry the highest risk first.

Conclusion

Risk assessments extend beyond mere vulnerability identification. They empower dealerships to develop a structured risk management framework, which includes preventive measures, contingency plans, and incident

---

[131] https://www.isaca.org/resources/news-and-trends/industry-news/2022/an-integrated-approach-to-security-audits.

response strategies. By quantifying risks, dealerships can make informed decisions to bolster their cybersecurity posture effectively.

Comprehensive security audits and risk assessments are pivotal for dealerships' cybersecurity resilience. The meticulous examination of network infrastructure, vulnerability scanning, and penetration testing ensure that vulnerabilities are proactively identified and addressed. On the other hand, risk assessments provide a structured methodology for understanding and prioritizing vulnerabilities, ultimately aiding in allocating resources to mitigate potential threats. By embracing these practices, dealerships can confidently navigate the intricate cybersecurity landscape, safeguarding their digital assets and ensuring the continuity of their operations.

B. SECURITY FRAMEWORKS AND COMPLIANCE ASSESSMENTS

These days, organizations must establish a solid foundation for their security measures. It necessitates the adoption of established security frameworks and undergoing periodic compliance assessments to ensure alignment with industry standards and regulatory requirements.

Exploring Security Frameworks

Security frameworks serve as comprehensive blueprints that guide organizations in designing, implementing, and managing effective cybersecurity measures. For dealerships seeking to fortify their cybersecurity defenses, several prominent frameworks provide invaluable guidance:

National Institute of Standards and Technology (NIST) Cybersecurity Framework

Developed by the US government, the NIST Cybersecurity Framework is a widely adopted guideline for enhancing cybersecurity resilience. It outlines a structured approach to identifying, protecting, detecting, responding to, and recovering from cyber threats. Dealerships can leverage this framework to create a customized cybersecurity strategy that aligns with their unique operational requirements.[132]

---

[132] https://www.pondurance.com/blog/ftc-safeguards-for-auto-dealerships/.

ISO/IEC 27001 Standard

The ISO/IEC 27001 standard is globally recognized as a benchmark for information security management systems (ISMS). By adopting ISO/IEC 27001, dealerships can establish a systematic approach to managing sensitive information and mitigating cybersecurity risks. The standard's holistic approach covers technical aspects and organizational and human factors, ensuring a comprehensive security posture.

Importance of Periodic Compliance Assessments

Compliance with industry standards and regulatory requirements is nonnegotiable in cybersecurity, especially in the highly regulated automotive sector. Periodic compliance assessments offer several crucial advantages.

- Ensuring adherence to standards: Industry standards and regulations are designed to address the dynamic nature of cyber threats. By conducting periodic compliance assessments, dealerships can verify their adherence to these evolving standards. This proactive approach helps organizations avoid potential vulnerabilities and ensures that their cybersecurity measures remain up to date.
- Mitigating legal and reputational risks: Noncompliance with industry regulations can result in severe legal consequences and damage the dealership's reputation. Compliance assessments provide a means to identify potential gaps in security measures and rectify them before they escalate into legal or reputational crises.
- Demonstrating commitment to security: In an era of increasing data breaches and cyber incidents, customers and partners seek reassurance that their information is handled securely. Periodic compliance assessments are tangible evidence of a dealership's commitment to cybersecurity. It can foster trust among stakeholders and potential customers, contributing to the dealership's credibility.
- Continuous improvement: Compliance assessments offer a feedback loop for continuous improvement. By identifying noncompliance or weaknesses in the security posture, dealerships can fine-tune their cybersecurity measures and enhance their overall resilience against cyber threats.

Conclusion

Adopting established security frameworks and the execution of periodic compliance assessments are essential pillars of robust cybersecurity for dealerships. Exploring frameworks like the NIST Cybersecurity Framework and ISO/IEC 27001 standard equips dealerships with structured guidelines for cybersecurity strategy formulation. Meanwhile, compliance assessments ensure adherence to evolving industry standards and regulations, safeguarding against legal risks and bolstering the organization's reputation. By embracing these practices, dealerships can proactively address cyber threats and establish themselves as trusted custodians of sensitive customer data.

C. ADDRESSING VULNERABILITIES AND IMPLEMENTING SECURITY RECOMMENDATIONS: A COMPREHENSIVE APPROACH

Addressing vulnerabilities and implementing security recommendations has become paramount for car dealerships to safeguard their digital assets, customer data, and reputation. With cyber threats becoming increasingly sophisticated and pervasive, dealerships must proactively identify vulnerabilities, assess risks, and implement robust security measures. This section delves into the multifaceted process of addressing vulnerabilities and highlights the importance of proactive security recommendations implementation.

Prioritizing Vulnerabilities Based on Risk

The first step in effective vulnerability management is prioritizing vulnerabilities based on their risk level. Not all vulnerabilities carry the same potential for exploitation or impact on the dealership's operations. Employing a risk assessment framework helps identify vulnerabilities that pose a significant threat and should be addressed on a priority basis. By considering factors, such as the potential consequences of exploitation, the likelihood of occurrence, and the assets at stake, dealerships can first allocate resources to tackle the most critical vulnerabilities. This approach ensures that limited resources are channeled where needed most, resulting in a more effective vulnerability management strategy.

Implementation of Security Recommendations

- Patch management: The software landscape is rife with vulnerabilities, and timely patch management is a fundamental practice to address known weaknesses. Dealerships should establish a well-structured patch management process encompassing identifying vulnerabilities, testing patches, and deploying them efficiently. Automated patch management tools can streamline this process, ensuring that security updates are applied promptly across all systems and applications. Regular patching mitigates known vulnerabilities and reduces the attack surface for cybercriminals.

- System hardening: System hardening involves tightening the security posture of software, operating systems, and devices by minimizing unnecessary functionalities and implementing security best practices. Dealerships should undertake thorough system hardening measures, such as turning off unused services, applying the principle of least privilege, and enforcing strong authentication mechanisms. System hardening fortifies the dealership's digital environment against a wide range of cyber threats by reducing the attack surface and potential avenues of exploitation.[133]

- Security awareness training: People remain one of the weakest links in the cybersecurity chain. Equipping dealership employees with the knowledge and skills to identify and respond to potential threats is crucial. Regular security awareness training programs educate employees about common cyber threats, social engineering tactics, and secure online practices. This empowers them to recognize phishing attempts, avoid clicking on malicious links, and promptly report unusual activities. With well-informed employees, dealerships create an additional layer of defense against cyber threats originating from human interactions.[134]

Continuous Improvement and Adaptation

The landscape of cybersecurity is dynamic, with new vulnerabilities emerging and threat actors employing innovative tactics. Therefore, addressing vulnerabilities and implementing security recommendations

---

[133] https://perception-point.io/guides/os-isolation/os-hardening-10-best-practices/.
[134] https://www.esecurityplanet.com/networks/patch-management-best-practices/.

must be an ongoing process. Regular security assessments, penetration testing, and vulnerability scanning are essential components of this process. Dealerships should continuously adapt their security measures to counteract evolving threats. This includes staying abreast of emerging vulnerabilities and threats, leveraging threat intelligence, and fine-tuning security measures based on changing circumstances.

Benefits of Effective Vulnerability Management

Implementing security recommendations and addressing vulnerabilities proactively offers numerous benefits that go beyond cybersecurity:

- Reduced risk exposure: Prioritizing vulnerabilities and implementing security measures reduces the dealership's risk exposure to cyber threats. This minimizes the likelihood of successful attacks and potential data breaches.
- Enhanced operational resilience: By proactively addressing vulnerabilities, dealerships enhance the resilience of their digital infrastructure. This resilience ensures that the impact is minimized even if an attack occurs and recovery is expedited.
- Regulatory compliance: Adhering to security recommendations and addressing vulnerabilities aligns with industry standards and regulations. This avoids potential legal penalties and fosters trust among customers and partners.
- Financial savings: Investing in vulnerability management early prevents costly security incidents that might lead to financial losses, legal liabilities, and reputational damage.
- Customer trust: A secure digital environment and proactive vulnerability management enhance customer trust. Customers are more likely to engage with dealerships that prioritize their data security.

Conclusion

Addressing vulnerabilities and implementing security recommendations is an ongoing commitment that necessitates proactive planning, vigilant execution, and continuous adaptation. By prioritizing vulnerabilities based on risk, applying timely patches, hardening systems, and fostering security awareness, dealerships create a fortified cybersecurity posture. This posture defends against cyber threats, underpins regulatory compliance, and strengthens customer trust. In an era where cyber threats are a constant, addressing vulnerabilities is not only a necessity but also a strategic imperative for the long-term success of car dealerships.

CHAPTER 16

CYBER INSURANCE: MANAGING FINANCIAL RISKS AND LIABILITIES

A. UNDERSTANDING THE BENEFITS AND COVERAGE OF CYBER INSURANCE

In the digital age, where cyber threats loom large and the consequences of a data breach or cyber incident can be financially devastating, cyber insurance has emerged as a crucial tool for car dealerships to manage financial risks and liabilities. This section sheds light on the comprehensive nature of cyber insurance, its benefits, coverage options, and role in mitigating the potential financial fallout.

The Rising Need for Cyber Insurance

As technology becomes increasingly intertwined with business operations, the risks associated with cyber incidents have grown exponentially. From data breaches and ransomware attacks to business interruption and legal liabilities, the financial implications of these events can be catastrophic. Cyber insurance has emerged as a proactive measure to provide financial protection and resilience in the face of these risks.

Comprehensive Coverage Options

Cyber insurance is not a one-size-fits-all solution; rather, it offers a suite of coverage options tailored to car dealerships' unique vulnerabilities and needs. One of the key components of cyber insurance is data breach response coverage. It covers the costs of responding to a data breach, including legal fees, forensic investigations, customer notifications, and credit monitoring services. Such coverage ensures that the dealership can swiftly address the aftermath of a breach while minimizing financial strain.

In addition to data breach response coverage, cyber insurance also extends to cover business interruption losses. In the event of a cyber incident that disrupts normal business operations, this coverage assists in mitigating revenue losses and operational expenses during the recovery period. Moreover, cyber insurance covers legal liabilities arising from customer data breaches, providing financial protection against lawsuits and regulatory fines.

Mitigating Financial Risks

The financial risks associated with cyber incidents can extend far beyond immediate financial losses. Data breaches can result in reputational damage, loss of customer trust, and even legal battles. Cyber insurance plays a pivotal role in mitigating these risks by providing financial support to navigate the aftermath of a cyber incident. This support empowers dealerships to respond effectively, compensate affected parties, and cover legal expenses, all of which contribute to maintaining the dealership's financial stability and reputation.

The Benefits of Cyber Insurance

The benefits of cyber insurance are manifold and extend beyond financial protection. First and foremost, cyber insurance provides peace of mind. It assures dealership stakeholders that the organization is equipped to manage the fallout without compromising its financial health in the event of a cyber incident. This assurance extends to customers, partners, and investors, enhancing trust and confidence in the dealership's operations. Let us elaborate further.[135]

Peace of Mind and Stakeholder Confidence

At the heart of the benefits offered by cyber insurance is the assurance of peace of mind. This peace of mind ripples across the dealership's ecosystem, from internal stakeholders to external partners, customers, and investors. Knowing that the dealership possesses a robust cyber insurance policy signifies a proactive approach to risk management. It demonstrates the dealership's preparedness to handle the aftermath of a cyber incident without compromising its financial stability.

Reinforcement of Risk Management Strategy

Cyber insurance isn't merely a financial safeguard but an integral part of the dealership's overall risk management strategy. By shifting the financial burden of cyber incidents to the insurer, dealerships can strategically allocate resources to bolster their cybersecurity measures. This strategic allocation is akin to investing in prevention rather than firefighting. By dedicating resources to preemptive cybersecurity measures, the dealership can significantly reduce the likelihood of incidents in the first place.

---

[135] https://www.nerdwallet.com/article/small-business/cybersecurity-insurance.

Commitment to Proactive Risk Mitigation

One of the key aspects of cyber insurance's benefits lies in its ability to highlight the dealership's commitment to proactive risk mitigation. Rather than relying solely on reactive responses to cyber threats, dealerships with cyber insurance communicate a proactive stance. This commitment trickles down to every facet of the dealership's operations, from training employees to implementing robust cybersecurity measures.

Conclusion

In an era where cyber threats are pervasive, and their financial repercussions can be severe, cyber insurance has emerged as a critical tool for car dealerships to safeguard their financial resilience. With comprehensive coverage options encompassing data breach response, business interruption, and legal liabilities, cyber insurance empowers dealerships to navigate the complex landscape of cyber incidents confidently. Beyond financial protection, cyber insurance offers peace of mind, enhances risk management strategies, and reinforces the dealership's commitment to proactive cybersecurity. Cyber insurance is a strategic investment in the dealership's long-term financial stability and success.

B. EVALUATING COVERAGE OPTIONS AND REQUIREMENTS FOR DEALERSHIPS

When safeguarding against the ever-evolving landscape of cyber threats, cyber insurance emerges as a critical tool in a dealership's arsenal. However, not all cyber insurance policies are created equal, and navigating the landscape of coverage options and requirements can be daunting. This section delves into the intricacies of evaluating cyber insurance coverage, providing dealerships with a road map to make informed decisions that align with their unique needs and risk profiles.

Factors to Consider

The evaluation process for cyber insurance begins with a comprehensive assessment of various factors. Dealerships must consider the specific nature of their operations, the volume of sensitive customer data they handle, their technological infrastructure, and the regulatory environment they operate within. Understanding these factors is paramount in selecting a policy that offers adequate coverage tailored to the dealership's requirements.

Policy Terms and Conditions

Every cyber insurance policy comes with its own set of terms and conditions. Dealerships must meticulously review these terms to understand what is covered and what is not. It includes understanding the scope of coverage, the types of cyber incidents covered (data breaches, ransomware attacks, etc.), and the specific financial limits associated with each type of incident.

Coverage Limits and Deductibles

Coverage limits and deductibles play a significant role in determining the effectiveness of a cyber insurance policy. Dealerships should analyze the coverage limits to ensure they align with potential financial losses from a cyber incident. Simultaneously, evaluating deductibles—the amount the dealership is responsible for paying before the insurance coverage kicks in—is essential in assessing the policy's affordability.

Assessment of Dealership-Specific Risks

One of the critical aspects of evaluating coverage options is assessing dealership-specific risks. This involves thoroughly examining the dealership's operations, data handling practices, and vulnerabilities. For instance, if the dealership relies heavily on online transactions, its risk exposure will differ from a dealership with primarily in-person sales. Identifying these unique risks enables the dealership to select a policy that directly addresses its vulnerabilities.

Understanding Policy Exclusions

Understanding what a cyber insurance policy does not cover is as important as understanding what it covers. Policy exclusions outline situations or events for which the policy will not provide coverage. These exclusions can range from certain cyberattacks to failure to meet specific security requirements. Dealerships should meticulously review these exclusions to avoid surprises when filing a claim.

Compliance and Regulatory Requirements

Dealerships operate within a regulatory landscape that governs data protection and cybersecurity. A robust cyber insurance policy should align with these regulatory requirements. Ensuring the policy meets compliance standards helps the dealership avoid legal and financial pitfalls.

Conclusion

Evaluating cyber insurance coverage options and requirements is not a one-size-fits-all endeavor. Rather, it's a tailored process that requires a deep understanding of the dealership's operations, risk landscape, and regulatory environment. By factoring in policy terms, coverage limits, deductibles, dealership-specific risks, and policy exclusions, dealerships can make empowered decisions that provide robust protection against cyber threats.

C. INSURANCE CLAIMS AND INCIDENT REPORTING PROCEDURES

As the automotive industry becomes increasingly digitalized, the importance of cyber insurance in protecting dealerships against potential cyber threats cannot be overstated. However, the efficacy of a cyber insurance policy lies not only in its coverage but also in the seamless process of filing claims and reporting incidents. This section provides car dealerships with a comprehensive understanding of the steps involved in making cyber insurance claims and reporting incidents, ensuring a swift and effective response when a cyber incident occurs.

Filing Cyber Insurance Claims

When a cyber incident strikes, prompt and accurate claim submission is essential to initiate recovery. Car dealerships should contact their cyber insurance provider's designated point of contact. This often involves contacting a claims representative or customer service hotline provided in the policy documentation. Dealerships must provide relevant details about the incident, such as the type of attack, the affected systems, and the extent of the damage.

Documentation and Evidence

A successful cyber insurance claim hinges on proper documentation and evidence. Dealerships should prepare a comprehensive incident report that includes a detailed account of the incident, the timeline of events, and the steps taken to mitigate the impact. Additionally, any communication with law enforcement agencies, third-party experts, or affected customers should be documented and included in the claim submission.

Compliance with Policy Requirements

Before filing a claim, reviewing the policy terms and conditions is imperative to ensure compliance with specific requirements. Some policies may have specific timeframes within which claims must be filed, and adhering to these deadlines can impact the claim's validity. Dealerships should also confirm that the incident falls within the scope of coverage outlined in the policy.

Incident Reporting Procedures

Timely incident reporting is essential for claim filing and compliance with policy requirements and potential legal obligations. Dealerships should establish a clear incident reporting process that involves notifying appropriate personnel within the organization, such as the IT team, senior management, and legal counsel. This ensures that the necessary measures are promptly taken to contain and address the incident.

Collaboration with Experts

Cyber insurance policies often require collaboration with cybersecurity experts and forensic investigators to assess the extent of the breach, identify vulnerabilities, and develop a remediation plan. Dealerships should have a network of cybersecurity professionals and legal advisors who can provide expert assistance during and after a cyber incident.

Continuous Communication

Open and transparent communication with the insurance provider is crucial throughout the claims and incident reporting process. Regular updates on the incident's progress, mitigation efforts, and any new developments help build trust and streamline the claims process.

Conclusion

Navigating the landscape of cyber insurance claims and incident reporting can be intricate. Still, with a well-defined process and proactive preparedness, car dealerships can effectively manage the aftermath of cyber incidents. By adhering to policy requirements, documenting incidents thoroughly, collaborating with experts, and maintaining open communication with insurance providers, dealerships can ensure a smoother path toward recovery.

CHAPTER 17

EMERGING TECHNOLOGIES AND FUTURE TRENDS IN DEALERSHIP CYBERSECURITY

A. IMPACT OF EMERGING TECHNOLOGIES ON DEALERSHIP CYBERSECURITY

As the automotive industry evolves at an unprecedented pace, propelled by cutting-edge technologies, car dealerships find themselves at the crossroads of innovation and cybersecurity challenges. The integration of emerging technologies, such as connected cars, autonomous vehicles, and artificial intelligence, has ushered in a new era of convenience, efficiency, and customer experiences. However, alongside these advancements, a host of cybersecurity implications have emerged, demanding a comprehensive understanding and proactive approach.

Connected Cars and IoT

Connected cars, fueled by the Internet of Things (IoT), enable seamless communication among vehicles, drivers, and external systems. While this connectivity enhances features like remote diagnostics and infotainment, it also introduces a wider attack surface. Malicious actors can exploit vulnerabilities in connected car systems, gaining unauthorized access to critical functions or harvesting sensitive data. Dealerships must prioritize robust encryption, intrusion detection systems, and continuous monitoring to safeguard against potential breaches.

Autonomous Vehicles and Safety Challenges

Autonomous vehicles promise a future of enhanced safety and efficiency, but their complex software and hardware components raise cybersecurity concerns. A breach in an autonomous vehicle's control systems could have catastrophic consequences. Dealerships must collaborate with manufacturers to ensure cybersecurity is integrated throughout the design and development stages, implementing secure coding practices and frequent security assessments.

Artificial Intelligence and Data Privacy

AI-powered applications are transforming customer experiences, from personalized recommendations to predictive maintenance. However, AI's reliance on massive datasets poses privacy risks if not managed appropriately. Dealerships must uphold data privacy regulations, such as GDPR or CCPA, and implement data anonymization techniques to protect customer information while leveraging AI's benefits.

Proactive Security Measures

To mitigate the risks associated with emerging technologies, dealerships must adopt proactive security measures. This includes robust network segmentation to prevent lateral movement by attackers, regular software updates to address vulnerabilities, and strong access controls to limit unauthorized system access.

Industry Collaboration and Standards

The dynamic landscape of emerging technologies requires collaboration across the automotive industry. Manufacturers, dealerships, and technology providers must work together to establish cybersecurity standards, share threat intelligence, and develop best practices. Industry-wide initiatives can foster a collective defense against evolving cyber threats.

Continuous Training and Awareness

As technology evolves, cybersecurity awareness and training become indispensable. Dealership staff should undergo regular training to stay updated on emerging threats, best practices, and incident response procedures. This human element is crucial in preventing social engineering attacks and ensuring a culture of cyber resilience.

Conclusion

As dealerships embrace the potential of emerging technologies, striking a balance between innovation and cybersecurity becomes paramount. The benefits of connected cars, autonomous vehicles, and AI-driven experiences are transformative, but robust cybersecurity strategies must underpin them. By understanding the unique risks associated with each technology and implementing proactive security measures, dealerships can thrive in the digital age while safeguarding customer trust and operational continuity.

B. EVOLVING REGULATORY LANDSCAPE AND COMPLIANCE CONSIDERATIONS

The regulatory framework governing cybersecurity is also transforming in the rapidly evolving digital landscape, where technology and innovation intertwine. Car dealerships, at the forefront of these changes, must navigate a complex web of emerging regulations and compliance considerations to ensure their cybersecurity practices align with legal requirements and industry standards.

The Cybersecurity Maturity Model Certification

The emergence of the Cybersecurity Maturity Model Certification (CMMC) represents a significant shift in regulatory focus. Developed by the US Department of Defense, the CMMC mandates a tiered approach to cybersecurity certification for contractors and suppliers handling sensitive defense information. Car dealerships engaged in defense contracts must now meet specified cybersecurity levels to protect critical data.[136]

International Data Protection Laws

As technology transcends borders, international data protection laws are increasingly relevant. Regulations, such as the General Data Protection Regulation in the European Union and the California Consumer Privacy Act, set global data privacy and protection standards. Even if dealerships don't directly operate in these regions, they may still need to comply when handling customer data originating from these jurisdictions.

Impact on Customer Trust

Compliance with evolving regulations is not merely a legal obligation; it's also a key component of building and maintaining customer trust. In an era of heightened data breaches and privacy concerns, customers are more conscious of how their data is handled. Dealerships demonstrating a commitment to compliance instill confidence in their customers and strengthen their brand reputation.

---

[136] https://learn.microsoft.com/en-us/azure/compliance/offerings/offering-cmmc.

Challenges of Changing Regulations

Navigating the evolving regulatory landscape poses challenges for dealerships. Staying up to date with new regulations, interpreting their implications, and implementing necessary changes promptly can be daunting. Noncompliance can result in penalties, reputational damage, and legal liabilities, emphasizing the criticality of proactive compliance strategies.

Opportunities for Enhancement

While regulatory changes present challenges, they also offer opportunities for enhancing cybersecurity. Regulations often set baseline security requirements, encouraging dealerships to bolster their security posture. By embracing these requirements as a starting point, dealerships can implement stronger security measures beyond compliance, improving overall resilience against cyber threats.

Continuous Adaptation

The evolving regulatory landscape necessitates a mindset of continuous adaptation. Regulatory changes are not static; they reflect the evolving threat landscape and the need for enhanced cybersecurity practices. Dealerships should establish mechanisms for ongoing monitoring of regulatory developments and assess how they impact their operations.

Conclusion

In a world where technological advancements and cybersecurity are inextricably linked, dealership cybersecurity must harmonize with the evolving regulatory landscape. Compliance is not an isolated task; it's an ongoing journey that requires vigilance, collaboration, and adaptation. Dealerships that view compliance as an opportunity for growth rather than a mere requirement can leverage emerging regulations to strengthen their cybersecurity foundations, enhance customer trust, and ensure their place in the secure future of the automotive industry. By forging ahead with a commitment to compliance and cybersecurity excellence, dealerships can confidently navigate the regulatory journey and seize the opportunities presented by the digital age.

C. PROACTIVE MEASURES AND CONTINUOUS IMPROVEMENT STRATEGIES

In the dynamic landscape of cybersecurity, where threats evolve rapidly, adopting a proactive stance and pursuing continuous improvement is paramount for car dealerships to safeguard their digital assets and customer trust. As the automotive industry embraces emerging technologies, dealerships must stay ahead of cyber threats through proactive measures and relentlessly enhancing their security posture.

Harnessing Threat Intelligence

Threat intelligence is the cornerstone of proactive cybersecurity. It involves collecting, analyzing, and leveraging information about cyber threats to anticipate and mitigate potential risks. Dealerships should establish mechanisms to gather intelligence about emerging threats, vulnerabilities, and attack patterns. This knowledge empowers them to take preemptive actions to defend against new and evolving threats.

Fostering Security Awareness

Human error remains a significant vulnerability in cybersecurity. Dealerships should invest in robust security awareness programs to educate employees about cyber threats, safe online practices, and the importance of following security protocols. An informed workforce is a powerful defense against phishing attacks, social engineering, and other tactics employed by cybercriminals.

Continuous Training Initiatives

Cyber threats are not static, and neither should training initiatives be. Regular and updated training programs are essential to equip employees with the latest knowledge and skills to combat evolving threats. Training should cover identifying phishing emails, using strong passwords, and recognizing suspicious activities.

Regular Risk Assessments

Cyber threats are not one-size-fits-all; they vary based on factors like technology, industry, and geography. Regular risk assessments tailored to the unique context of dealerships are essential. These assessments help identify vulnerabilities, prioritize risks, and allocate resources effectively to address the most critical security gaps.

Penetration Testing for Resilience

Penetration testing, often called ethical hacking, is a proactive strategy that assesses the effectiveness of existing security measures by simulating cyberattacks. Dealerships can employ experienced cybersecurity professionals to simulate real-world attack scenarios and identify weaknesses that need strengthening.

Embracing the Cycle of Improvement

Cybersecurity is not a one-time project; it's a continuous improvement journey. Dealerships should establish a cycle of improvement that includes regular updates to security policies, procedures, and technologies. This cycle ensures the cybersecurity strategy remains aligned with emerging threats and industry best practices.

Collaboration and Knowledge Sharing

The landscape of cyber threats is complex and ever-changing. Dealerships can benefit from collaboration with industry peers, sharing insights, best practices, and lessons learned. By participating in cybersecurity forums, conferences, and industry groups, dealerships can tap into collective knowledge to enhance their defenses.

Conclusion

In an era of rapid technological advancements and sophisticated cyber threats, dealership cybersecurity must transcend reactive measures and embrace proactive strategies. By fostering a vigilance, continuous improvement, and collaboration culture, dealerships can position themselves as defenders against emerging cyber risks. As the automotive landscape evolves with technologies like connected cars and autonomous vehicles, the commitment to cybersecurity becomes a growth catalyst, instilling customer trust, ensuring regulatory compliance, and securing the industry's future. By taking proactive measures, investing in ongoing training, and staying adaptable, dealerships can forge ahead confidently into the exciting yet challenging landscape of emerging technologies and evolving cyber threats.

CHAPTER 18

CONCLUSION AND ROAD MAP FOR DEALERSHIP CYBERSECURITY

A. RECAP OF KEY POINTS AND TAKEAWAYS

As we conclude this comprehensive guide to dealership cybersecurity, it's essential to recap the key points and takeaways that emphasize cybersecurity's critical role in safeguarding the automotive industry's digital landscape. Throughout this guide, we have explored the various dimensions of cybersecurity, ranging from understanding threats to implementing strategies for resilience.

Here's a recap of the key insights and takeaways:

Importance of Dealership Cybersecurity

Cybersecurity is not just a matter of compliance; it's crucial for protecting customer data, maintaining trust, and ensuring business continuity. The automotive industry's increasing digitization exposes dealerships to cyber threats that can have severe financial and reputational consequences.

Common Threats Faced

Dealerships encounter many threats, including data breaches, ransomware attacks, phishing, and insider threats. The interconnectedness of automotive systems introduces vulnerabilities that hackers exploit to gain unauthorized access.

Strategies to Mitigate Risks

Implementing multilayered security measures, including firewalls, intrusion detection systems, and endpoint protection solutions, is essential to create robust defense mechanisms. Secure coding practices, employee training, and incident response planning are crucial elements of a comprehensive cybersecurity strategy. Regular security audits, compliance assessments, and risk management help identify vulnerabilities and prioritize mitigation efforts.

Ongoing Vigilance and Continuous Improvement

Cyber threats evolve rapidly, demanding constant vigilance and proactive measures. The landscape of dealership cybersecurity is dynamic, with emerging technologies and evolving regulations requiring continuous adaptation.

Building a Culture of Cybersecurity

Creating a culture of cybersecurity is as important as implementing technical measures. Employee training, security awareness programs, and collaboration across the organization contribute to a proactive cybersecurity mindset.

Collaboration and Industry Initiatives

Dealerships can benefit from collaborating with industry peers, sharing insights, and participating in cybersecurity forums to stay updated on the latest threats and best practices.

Regulatory Landscape and Compliance

Various regulations, including the Fair Credit Reporting Act, Truth in Lending Act, and Gramm-Leach-Bliley Act, impose requirements on dealerships regarding data protection, transparency, and consumer rights. The Federal Trade Commission enforces cybersecurity practices and ensures fair and ethical business conduct.

Conclusion

In a landscape where technology accelerates progress and introduces risks, cybersecurity becomes the foundation for the automotive industry's future. Dealerships play a pivotal role in this ecosystem, protecting customer data, enabling digital innovation, and building customer trust.

B. IMPORTANCE OF A HOLISTIC APPROACH TO DEALERSHIP CYBERSECURITY

In dealership cybersecurity, a holistic approach is the cornerstone of a robust defense against the multifaceted landscape of cyber threats. Such an approach transcends isolated measures and addresses cybersecurity as a comprehensive and integrated strategy encompassing various aspects of the dealership's operations.

Technical Measures

Technical defenses, such as firewalls, intrusion detection systems, and encryption protocols, form the first defense against cyber intrusions. These measures create digital barriers that deter unauthorized access and data breaches. However, more than technical measures is required; they must be part of a larger, well-coordinated effort.

Employee Training

Employees are both the users and gatekeepers of a dealership's digital ecosystem. Cybersecurity education and training are paramount in cultivating a vigilant and security-conscious workforce. By ensuring that employees understand the threats and recognize suspicious activities, dealerships can reduce the risk of successful phishing attempts and other social engineering tactics.

Vendor Management

Modern dealerships often rely on a network of vendors and third-party service providers. These entities can inadvertently introduce vulnerabilities if not vetted and monitored properly. A holistic cybersecurity approach involves robust vendor risk management practices to ensure that external partners adhere to security standards and practices.

Regulatory Compliance

Compliance with regulations, such as the Fair Credit Reporting Act, Truth in Lending Act, Gramm-Leach-Bliley Act, and others, is not just a legal requirement but a foundational pillar of cybersecurity. Meeting regulatory standards ensures customer data is handled responsibly and ethically, safeguarding the dealership and its clientele.

Collaboration and Industry Partnerships

Dealerships do not operate in isolation. Collaboration and partnerships with industry peers, cybersecurity organizations, and law enforcement agencies create a collective defense mechanism. Sharing threat intelligence, best practices, and lessons learned strengthens the automotive ecosystem's resilience against cyber threats.

Risk Assessment and Mitigation

A holistic approach involves continuous risk assessment to identify vulnerabilities and assess potential impacts. By understanding the dealership's unique risk landscape, cybersecurity measures can be tailored to address specific threats effectively. Mitigation strategies can then be prioritized based on the assessed risks.

Incident Response Planning

Despite preventive measures, incidents may occur. A well-defined incident response plan ensures the dealership can minimize damage and recover swiftly. This plan encompasses technical remediation and communication strategies to manage reputational risks.

Cyber Insurance

While not a substitute for preventive measures, cyber insurance can provide a safety net during a cyber incident. A holistic cybersecurity approach includes evaluating and obtaining appropriate cyber insurance coverage to mitigate potential financial losses.

Adaptation to Emerging Technologies

A holistic approach to cybersecurity becomes even more critical as the automotive industry embraces emerging technologies like connected cars, autonomous vehicles, and AI-driven systems. These technologies introduce novel attack vectors that require proactive security measures.

Conclusion

A dealership's cybersecurity posture is only as strong as its weakest link. A holistic approach recognizes that cybersecurity is not confined to firewalls and software; it's an overarching philosophy that infuses every aspect of the dealership's operations. By integrating technical defenses, employee education, regulatory compliance, vendor management, and collaborative efforts, dealerships can establish a resilient defense against the evolving and complex landscape of cyber threats. Through this holistic lens, dealerships can confidently navigate the digital future, secure in the knowledge that they are well-prepared to safeguard their operations, customers, and industry standing.

C. ROAD MAP FOR DEALERSHIP CYBERSECURITY IMPLEMENTATION

Creating a robust cybersecurity strategy for your dealership involves several key steps, each designed to strengthen your defenses, enhance awareness, and ensure compliance. This road map outlines the process comprehensively to guide you through the implementation process:

Assess Current State and Identify Assets

Evaluate your dealership's digital assets, including customer information, financial records, and communication systems. Identify critical business processes and dependencies on digital infrastructure and data flows to understand how sensitive information is collected, processed, and stored.

Develop a Comprehensive Cybersecurity Strategy

Formulate a comprehensive cybersecurity strategy that aligns with your dealership's objectives. Define the scope of your cybersecurity efforts, encompassing technical, procedural, and human aspects. Set *smart* goals to guide your strategy's implementation.

Conduct a Detailed Risk Assessment

Perform a thorough risk assessment to identify potential threats and vulnerabilities to your dealership. Evaluate the potential impact and likelihood of various threats to prioritize mitigation efforts. Consider conducting threat modeling to anticipate and prepare for potential attack scenarios.

Implement Technical Controls with Precision

Deploy advanced firewall systems to monitor incoming and outgoing network traffic effectively. In real time, utilize intrusion detection/prevention systems to identify and respond to potential cyber threats. Establish stringent network segmentation to limit the lateral movement of attackers within your infrastructure.

Foster a Security-Conscious Culture

Develop an ongoing cybersecurity training program for all employees, including sales, service, and administrative staff. Educate them about the significance of cybersecurity, common social engineering tactics, and the importance of reporting suspicious activities. Conduct simulated phishing exercises to enhance employees' awareness.

Navigate the Regulatory Landscape

Understand relevant regulations, such as the FCRA, TILA, and GLBA, and their implications on your dealership's cybersecurity practices. Establish processes and policies to ensure compliance with customer data privacy requirements. Regularly review and update your cybersecurity practices to remain aligned with evolving regulations.

Develop a Detailed Incident Response Plan

Create a well-defined incident response plan that outlines procedures for detecting, assessing, and responding to cybersecurity incidents. Assign specific roles and responsibilities within the incident response team and define escalation paths. Conduct regular tabletop exercises to test your incident response procedures' effectiveness.

Establish Vendor Risk Management

Implement a robust vendor risk management program to assess the cybersecurity posture of third-party vendors and suppliers. Regularly review contracts and agreements to ensure they meet cybersecurity standards and compliance requirements. Establish communication channels for reporting and addressing cybersecurity incidents involving vendors.

Embrace Ongoing Monitoring and Continuous Assessment

Implement a security information and event management system to monitor network activities and identify potential security breaches. Perform regular vulnerability assessments and penetration testing to identify and address vulnerabilities in your dealership's systems proactively.

Adapt to the Dynamic Threat Landscape

Stay updated on emerging cyber threats, tactics, and techniques relevant to the automotive industry. Participate in information-sharing forums, industry groups, and cybersecurity conferences to gain insights from peers and experts.

Collaborate to Strengthen the Industry

Engage in collaborative initiatives within the automotive industry to share threat intelligence and best practices. Collaborate with industry associations, manufacturers, and cybersecurity organizations to collectively enhance cybersecurity resilience.

Incorporate Cyber Insurance

Evaluate your dealership's risk profile to determine the appropriate level of cyber insurance coverage. Understand your cyber insurance policy's terms, coverage limits, and exclusions to ensure alignment with your dealership's needs.

Conclusion

This road map provides a structured approach to building a resilient cybersecurity posture for your dealership. Following these steps demonstrates your commitment to protecting customer data, maintaining regulatory compliance, and proactively defending against cyber threats. As the cybersecurity landscape evolves, this road map guides you toward continuous improvement and adaptation, ensuring your dealership's sustained cybersecurity excellence.

EPILOGUE

As we conclude our journey through the pages of *Automotive Dealership Safeguard: A Comprehensive Guide to Cybersecurity and Financial Compliance,* we stand at the threshold of a new era. An era where the automotive industry is not just defined by the vehicles it produces but also by the strength of its cybersecurity defenses.

This book has been a companion on that transformative journey. It has illuminated the complexities of financial regulations, unveiled operational vulnerabilities, and provided us with robust strategies to fortify data protection. It has emphasized the critical role of employee awareness and the need for a delicate balance when embracing emerging technologies. It has guided us through the legal frameworks and ISO standards, offering us a compass to navigate the complex landscape of cybersecurity.

But it doesn't end here. The knowledge we've gained from these pages is a torch that will continue to light our way into the future. Cybersecurity is not a destination; it's a journey, an ongoing effort that demands constant vigilance and adaptation.

As we move forward, remember the lessons learned from "Automotive Dealership Safeguard." Let us implement the best practices and frameworks it has advocated. Let us proactively manage risks and embrace change with confidence. Let us safeguard our operations and leverage cybersecurity as a catalyst for growth and innovation.

The future of automotive dealerships is intertwined with the future of cybersecurity. By embracing the principles and insights shared in this book, we are not just securing success but shaping it. As we embark on this journey, let us do so with a renewed sense of purpose and a commitment to building a safer, more resilient future for our industry.

GLOSSARY

- Access control: Managing and enforcing user permissions to access resources based on their roles, responsibilities, and authentication.
- Advanced persistent threat: A targeted and prolonged cyberattack by sophisticated threat actors aiming to gain unauthorized access to sensitive information.
- Artificial intelligence: Advanced technology imitating human intelligence, enhancing cybersecurity through automation, anomaly detection, and threat analysis.
- Biometric authentication: Using unique biological characteristics, such as fingerprints or facial recognition, to verify a user's identity.
- Black hat hacker: An individual or group who engages in malicious and unauthorized activities to exploit vulnerabilities for personal gain or malicious intent.
- Blockchain technology: A distributed and decentralized digital ledger that records transactions securely and tamper-resistantly, often associated with cryptocurrencies.
- Blockchain: A decentralized and tamper-resistant digital ledger used for secure and transparent recording of transactions.
- Botnet: A network of compromised computers, or bots, controlled by an attacker to perform coordinated actions, such as launching DDoS attacks.
- Bug bounty program: An initiative where organizations reward individuals for identifying and reporting system security vulnerabilities.
- Business continuity planning: A strategy outlining measures to ensure an organization's critical functions continue in the face of disruptive events or disasters.
- Cloud access security broker (CASB): A security solution that provides visibility and control over data and applications accessed through cloud services.
- Cloud security: Measures and strategies to protect data, applications, and systems in cloud environments, ensuring data privacy and compliance.

- Compliance assessment: Evaluation of an organization's adherence to industry regulations and standards to ensure cybersecurity and data protection.
- Connected cars: Vehicles with internet connectivity and communication capabilities enable data exchange and remote control.
- Consumer data privacy laws: Regulations designed to protect individuals' personal information from unauthorized access, use, or disclosure.
- Credential stuffing: An attack where attackers use stolen usernames and passwords from one breach to gain unauthorized access to other accounts.
- Critical infrastructure: Essential systems and assets, such as energy, transportation, and water, that if disrupted can have severe consequences.
- Cryptography: Using mathematical techniques to secure communication and data through encryption, decryption, and digital signatures.
- Cryptography: Using mathematical techniques to secure communication and data, including encryption and decryption.
- Cyber hygiene: Good cybersecurity practices, such as keeping software up to date, using strong passwords, and avoiding suspicious links.
- Cyber insurance: A type of insurance coverage that helps organizations mitigate financial losses from cyber incidents, including data breaches, cyberattacks, and business interruptions.
- Cyber insurance: Coverage that helps organizations manage financial losses and liabilities from cyberattacks and data breaches.
- Cyber threat intelligence: Information about potential and existing cybersecurity threats is collected, analyzed, and used to make informed decisions about security measures.
- Cyber threat intelligence: Information about potential cyber threats, including tactics, techniques, and indicators, used to predict and prevent attacks.
- Cybersecurity framework: A set of guidelines, best practices, and standards to help organizations establish effective cybersecurity controls and risk management strategies.
- Cybersecurity framework: A structured approach to managing cybersecurity risks, often provided by recognized standards like NIST's Cybersecurity Framework.

- Cybersecurity governance: The framework and processes for establishing, implementing, and monitoring cybersecurity policies and practices within an organization.
- Cybersecurity maturity model certification: A framework developed by the US Department of Defense to assess and enhance the cybersecurity practices of defense contractors.
- Cybersecurity maturity model certification: A framework for measuring and certifying the cybersecurity capabilities of contractors working with the US Department of Defense.
- Cybersecurity policy: A formal document outlining an organization's rules, guidelines, and procedures for protecting information and technology assets.
- Cybersecurity: Comprehensive measures and practices to safeguard digital systems, networks, and data from cyber threats and unauthorized access.
- Dark web: A hidden part of the internet not indexed by traditional search engines, often used for illegal activities.
- Data breach: Unauthorized access, acquisition, or disclosure of sensitive or confidential information, often leading to privacy breaches and potential harm to individuals.
- Data breach: Unauthorized intrusion into computer systems or networks, resulting in the exposure, theft, or compromise of sensitive information.
- Data classification: The process of categorizing data based on its sensitivity, value, and importance to apply appropriate security controls and protection measures.
- Data encryption: The process of converting data into a code to protect its confidentiality and integrity, ensuring only authorized parties can access it.
- Data loss prevention: Technologies and strategies to prevent unauthorized access, transmission, or leakage of sensitive or confidential data.
- Data masking: A technique that substitutes sensitive data with fictional or scrambled values, preserving data integrity while protecting confidentiality.
- Decryption: Converting encrypted data to its original, readable form using an encryption key.

- Digital forensics: Collecting, analyzing, and preserving digital evidence to investigate and respond to cybercrimes.
- Digital forensics: Collecting, preserving, analyzing, and presenting digital evidence to investigate and respond to cybercrimes and security incidents.
- Digital identity: The digital representation of an individual or entity used for online authentication and authorization.
- Disaster recovery: Restoring and recovering data, applications, and systems after a disruptive event, minimizing downtime and data loss.
- Distributed denial of service attack: An attack where multiple compromised systems overwhelm a target system with a flood of traffic, causing it to become unavailable.
- Eavesdropping: Unauthorized interception and communication monitoring between parties, often for gathering sensitive information.
- Emerging technologies: Newly developed or gaining prominence, such as artificial intelligence, Internet of Things, and blockchain.
- Encryption algorithm: A mathematical formula that transforms data into ciphertext and vice versa, ensuring data confidentiality.
- Encryption key: A cryptographic code used to encrypt and decrypt data, ensuring secure communication and protection of sensitive information.
- Endpoint security: Protection of devices, including computers and mobiles, from cyber threats through antivirus, firewalls, and intrusion prevention systems.
- Firewall: A network security device or software that monitors and controls incoming and outgoing network traffic, acting as a barrier between trusted and untrusted networks.
- Firmware: Software that is embedded in hardware devices, controlling their functionality and behavior.
- General data protection regulation: European Union regulation designed to protect individuals' personal data and privacy rights within the EU.
- Gray hat hacker: Individuals who operate between ethical and unethical hacking, sometimes breaching systems without authorization but with good intentions.
- Hacker group: A collective of individuals collaborating on cyberattacks, often sharing tools, techniques, and resources.

- Holistic approach: Comprehensive strategy addressing all aspects of cybersecurity, considering technical, procedural, human, and regulatory factors.
- Honeynet: A network of intentionally vulnerable systems designed to attract and monitor cyberattacks' activities.
- Honeypot: A deceptive system or network designed to attract cyberattacks and gather information about their methods and tactics.
- Identity and access management: Systematic control of user identities, authentication, and authorization to ensure secure and appropriate data access.
- Incident notification: The process of informing affected parties about a cybersecurity incident, often required by regulations and industry standards.
- Incident response plan: A documented strategy outlining the steps and actions to take when responding to a cybersecurity incident.
- Incident response: A structured approach to managing and mitigating the aftermath of a cybersecurity incident, involving steps, such as identification, containment, eradication, recovery, and lessons learned.
- Incident triage: The initial assessment of a cybersecurity incident to determine its severity, impact, and appropriate response actions.
- Information security officer (ISO): A senior-level executive overseeing an organization's security strategy and implementation.
- Insider threat: A cybersecurity risk posed by individuals within an organization who misuse their access to cause harm or leak sensitive information.
- Internet of Things: A network of interconnected physical devices, vehicles, appliances, and other objects that collect and exchange data.
- Intrusion detection system: A security tool that monitors network traffic for suspicious activities or unauthorized access attempts and alerts administrators to potential threats.
- Intrusion prevention system: A security mechanism beyond detection by actively blocking or mitigating potential intrusions or attacks on a network or system.
- ISO 21434: International standard addressing automotive cybersecurity, providing guidelines and requirements for securing vehicles and components.

- ISO/IEC 27001: An international standard for information security management systems that outlines best practices for establishing, implementing, and maintaining security controls.
- Keylogger: Malware that records keystrokes to capture sensitive information, often used to steal passwords and confidential data.
- Machine learning: A subset of artificial intelligence that enables systems to learn and improve from experience, often used in cybersecurity for threat detection.
- Malware detection: Identifying and eliminating malware infections within systems and networks using antivirus and antimalware tools.
- Malware: Short for "malicious software," it refers to any software specifically designed to harm, exploit, or compromise computer systems and networks.
- Man-in-the-middle (MitM) attack: An attack where an attacker intercepts communication between two parties, often to eavesdrop or manipulate data.
- Mobile device management: Solutions and policies to manage and secure mobile devices within an organization, including remote wiping and encryption.
- Multifactor authentication: A security method that requires users to provide multiple forms of identification, such as passwords, tokens, and biometrics, to access a system or application.
- Network segmentation: Dividing a network into smaller segments to control traffic flow and enhance security by preventing lateral movement of attackers.
- NIST cybersecurity framework: A set of guidelines and best practices developed by the National Institute of Standards and Technology to improve cybersecurity risk management.
- NIST framework: The National Institute of Standards and Technology's guidelines provide a structured approach to managing and mitigating cybersecurity risks.
- Packet sniffing: The practice of capturing and analyzing network traffic to intercept data, often used for unauthorized surveillance or data theft.
- Patch management: Planning, implementing, and monitoring updates to software and systems to address security vulnerabilities and improve functionality.

- Payload: The malicious component of malware that performs unauthorized actions on a victim's system, such as data theft or system disruption.
- Payment Card Industry Data Security Standard: Framework ensuring secure handling of credit card data to prevent breaches and fraud.
- Penetration testing: "Ethical hacking" involves simulating cyberattacks to identify vulnerabilities and weaknesses in a system's defenses.
- Phishing: A type of cyberattack where attackers use deceptive tactics, often through emails or web sites, to trick users into revealing sensitive information or performing malicious actions.
- Point-to-point encryption: A security measure that encrypts payment card data from the point of capture until it reaches the secure processing environment.
- Privacy impact assessment: An assessment of the potential privacy risks and impacts associated with collecting and processing personal data.
- Privileged access management: Managing and controlling access to privileged accounts and information to prevent unauthorized access and potential misuse.
- Public key infrastructure (PKI): A framework that manages digital keys and certificates to provide secure authentication and communication.
- Ransomware: A type of malware that encrypts a victim's data, demanding a ransom payment for the decryption key, often causing significant disruptions.
- Ransomware: Malicious software that encrypts a victim's data, demanding a ransom payment in exchange for the decryption key.
- Red team and blue team: A simulated cybersecurity exercise where the "red team" plays the role of attackers and the "blue team" defends against their tactics, helping to identify vulnerabilities.
- Red team: A group of skilled cybersecurity professionals who simulate cyberattacks to assess an organization's defenses.
- Regulatory compliance: The adherence to laws, regulations, and standards relevant to an industry or sector, ensuring that organizations meet legal requirements and avoid penalties.
- Risk assessment: The evaluation of potential threats, vulnerabilities, and potential impacts to determine the level of risk and prioritize mitigation efforts.

- Role-based access control (RBAC): A security model that restricts system access based on users' roles, ensuring only authorized actions are performed.
- Rootkit: Malicious software designed to gain unauthorized access and control over a computer system, often hiding its presence from detection.
- Secure coding: Writing software code with security in mind, reducing vulnerabilities and potential attack surfaces.
- Secure DevOps: Integrating security practices into the DevOps development process to ensure that applications and systems are developed with security in mind.
- Secure payment gateway: An e-commerce service that securely authorizes and processes payment transactions between customers and merchants.
- Secure sockets layer/transport layer security: Cryptographic protocols that provide secure communication over networks commonly used for web sites.
- Security audit: A systematic evaluation of an organization's security measures, controls, and policies to assess compliance and identify vulnerabilities.
- Security awareness program: A structured initiative to educate employees and users about cybersecurity risks, best practices, and safe behaviors.
- Security awareness training: Educational programs that teach employees about cybersecurity best practices, threats, and how to recognize and respond to potential risks.
- Security baseline: A predefined level of security controls, configurations, and policies that serve as a starting point for secure system deployment.
- Security culture: The collective attitudes, behaviors, and practices of an organization's members toward cybersecurity.
- Security frameworks: Comprehensive guidelines, best practices, and standards for establishing effective cybersecurity controls and risk management strategies.
- Security incident and event management: A software solution that collects, analyzes, and correlates security event data from various sources to identify and respond to threats.
- Security incident response team: A dedicated team responsible for coordinating and leading an organization's response to cybersecurity incidents.

- Security incident: Any event compromising the confidentiality, integrity, or availability of information or systems, requiring investigation and response.
- Security information and event management: A software solution that collects, analyzes, and correlates security event data to detect and respond to threats.
- Security information sharing: Exchanging threat intelligence and security insights among organizations to enhance collective cybersecurity.
- Security operations center analyst: A cybersecurity professional responsible for monitoring and responding to security incidents in a SOC environment.
- Security operations center: A centralized team responsible for real-time monitoring, detecting, and responding to security incidents.
- Security patch: A software update designed to fix vulnerabilities and security flaws in applications, operating systems, and devices.
- Security posture: The overall strength and effectiveness of an organization's cybersecurity measures and controls.
- Security token service: A component that issues and manages security tokens for authentication and authorization.
- Security token: A physical or digital device used to authenticate users, providing an additional layer of security beyond passwords.
- Session hijacking: Unauthorized access to a user's active session, often by stealing session tokens or cookies.
- Single point of failure: A component or system whose failure can disrupt the entire network or system.
- Single sign-on: A system that allows users to access multiple applications or services with a single set of credentials, enhancing security and convenience.
- Social engineering: Psychological manipulation used by attackers to deceive individuals into divulging sensitive information or performing actions.
- Social engineering: Manipulating individuals into divulging confidential information or performing actions that compromise security through psychological tactics.
- Software patch: A piece of code used to update or fix vulnerabilities in software, enhancing security and performance.
- Supply chain security: Ensuring the security of products, components, and services throughout an organization's supply chain.

- Third-party risk management: The process of evaluating and managing the cybersecurity risks posed by third-party vendors, suppliers, and partners in an organization's ecosystem.
- Threat hunting: Proactively searching for signs of undetected threats within an organization's systems and networks.
- Threat intelligence: Information about potential and existing cybersecurity threats is collected, analyzed, and used to make informed decisions about security measures.
- Threat modeling: Identifying and evaluating potential software vulnerabilities during the development lifecycle to enhance security measures.
- Tokenization: The process of replacing sensitive data with unique tokens with no intrinsic value to protect data during transactions and storage.
- Trojan horse: Malicious software disguised as legitimate programs, tricking users into installing them, often leading to unauthorized access or data theft.
- Two-factor authentication: A security method requiring users to provide two types of authentication, enhancing account security.
- User behavior analytics: The analysis of user activities and behaviors to detect anomalies and potential security threats based on deviations from normal patterns.
- User behavior analytics: The analysis of user activities and behaviors to detect anomalies and potential security threats based on deviations from normal patterns.
- Vendor management: Overseeing and controlling relationships with third-party vendors to ensure they meet security and performance requirements.
- Virtual private network: A secure network connection that allows users to access the internet securely, encrypting data and masking IP addresses.
- Virtual private network: A secure network connection that encrypts data traffic, often used to ensure privacy and anonymity online.
- Virus: A malicious software that can replicate and attach itself to legitimate programs, spreading infections to other systems.
- Vulnerability assessment: Identifying and assessing security vulnerabilities in systems, applications, and networks to determine potential risks and prioritize remediation efforts.

- Vulnerability management: Identifying, assessing, and mitigating vulnerabilities in systems, applications, and networks.
- White hat hacker: Ethical hackers who use their skills to identify and fix security vulnerabilities, often employed by organizations to enhance cybersecurity.
- Whitelist and blacklist: A whitelist includes trusted entities or items, while a blacklist includes unauthorized or malicious ones, often used in access control.
- Worm: A self-replicating malware that spreads across networks by exploiting vulnerabilities without requiring user interaction.
- Zero-trust architecture: A security model that assumes no implicit trust within or outside an organization's network, verifying all users and devices.
- Zero-day vulnerability: A security vulnerability in software or hardware that attackers exploit before a vendor releases a patch or fix.

BIBLIOGRAPHY

- http://www.forvis.com/article/2022/07/dealerships-comply-ftc-data-breach-safeguards
- https://abdalslam.com/car-dealer-statistics
- https://advantagegps.com/wp-content/uploads/2022/09/P4C-White-Paper-FTC-Safeguards-Rule-Update-June-2022-FINAL.pdf
- https://airiam.com/auto-dealerships-cybersecurity/
- https://arcticwolf.com/resources/blog/car-dealerships-dealers-must-bolster-data-security-under-new-ftc-rule/
- https://arcticwolf.com/resources/blog/why-auto-dealers-are-prime-targets-for-ransomware-attacks/
- https://blog.checkpoint.com/security/a-german-car-attack-on-german-vehicle-businesses/
- https://blog.rsisecurity.com/your-third-party-cyber-risk-assessment-checklist/
- https://blog.sellyautomotive.com/blog/what-used-car-dealerships-must-do-to-comply-with-new-ftc-requirements-a-blog-about-what-ftc-compliance-means-for-automotive-dealers
- https://citrixready.citrix.com/content/dam/ready/program/secure-remote-access-program/pdf-censornetmfaadvancednetscalerguide-web.pdf
- https://collegegrad.com/industries/automobile-dealers
- https://contentsecurity.com.au/managed-cyber-security-awareness-program/
- https://csrc.nist.gov/CSRC/media/Events/Federal-Information-Systems-Security-Educators-As/documents/9.pdf
- https://csrc.nist.gov/Projects/Access-Control-Policy-and-Implementation-Guides
- https://cybersecurity.att.com/blogs/security-essentials/endpoint-protection-explained
- https://dealersocket.com/products/crm/
- https://digitaldealer.com/dealer-ops-leadership/four-cybersecurity-basics-must-haves-auto-dealerships/
- https://eandt.theiet.org/content/articles/2023/05/is-your-car-safe-from-a-cyber-attack/
- https://en.wikipedia.org/wiki/Phishing

- https://files.consumerfinance.gov/f/documents/201908_cfpb_automobile-finance-examination-procedures.pdf
- https://gatefy.com/blog/real-and-famous-cases-social-engineering-attacks/
- https://hbr.org/2021/05/is-third-party-software-leaving-you-vulnerable-to-cyberattacks
- https://ideas.repec.org/a/aza/jdpp00/y2019v2i4p362-367.html
- https://ieeexplore.ieee.org/abstract/document/8854548
- https://ieeexplore.ieee.org/document/7904776
- https://ieeexplore.ieee.org/document/8615162
- https://insights.sei.cmu.edu/blog/cybersecurity-architecture-part-2-system-boundary-and-boundary-protection/
- https://journals.sagepub.com/doi/pdf/10.1177/21582440211000049
- https://jumpcloud.com/blog/passwordless-authentication-vs-multi-factor-authentication
- https://learn.microsoft.com/en-us/azure/compliance/offerings/offering-cmmc
- https://learn.saylor.org/mod/book/view.php?id=29612&chapterid=5160
- https://leb.fbi.gov/articles/featured-articles/social-media-establishing-criteria-for-law-enforcement-use
- https://leb.fbi.gov/articles/featured-articles/social-media-establishing-criteria-for-law-enforcement-use
- https://link.springer.com/article/10.1007/s42154-021-00140-6
- https://link.springer.com/article/10.1186/s42400-019-0038-7
- https://link.springer.com/chapter/10.1007/978-3-319-58424-9_35
- https://link.springer.com/chapter/10.1007/978-3-642-28920-0_4
- https://mcmcpa.com/ftc-cyber-regulation-changes-for-auto-dealerships/
- https://media.defense.gov/2022/Jun/15/2003018261/-1/-1/0/CTR_NSA_NETWORK_INFRASTRUCTURE_SECURITY_GUIDE_20220615.PDF
- https://niada.com/dashboard/changes-to-the-safeguards-rule-and-how-it-applies-to-your-dealership/
- https://nvlpubs.nist.gov/nistpubs/ir/2021/NIST.IR.8276.pdf
- https://perception-point.io/guides/os-isolation/os-hardening-10-best-practices/
- https://securityintelligence.com/posts/marketing-public-relations-incident-response/
- https://socradar.io/automotive-industry-under-ransomware-attacks/

- https://support.microsoft.com/en-us/windows/device-encryption-in-windows-ad5dcf4b-dbe0-2331-228f-7925c2a3012d
- https://techbeacon.com/security/6-ways-develop-security-culture-top-bottom
- https://thedefenceworks.com/blog/the-benefits-of-using-phishing-simulations/
- https://us.norton.com/blog/how-to/the-importance-of-general-software-updates-and-patches
- https://www.alert-software.com/blog/incident-management-communication
- https://www.aspentechpolicyhub.org/wp-content/uploads/2020/06/Vendor-Cybersecurity-Contract-Language.pdf
- https://www.atlassian.com/incident-management/incident-communication
- https://www.autoremarketing.com/ar/84-percent-buyers-would-shun-their-dealership-after-data-breach/
- https://www.bankrate.com/loans/auto-loans/dealer-financing/
- https://www.bing.com/search?q=Business+System+Vulnerabilities+automotive+industry&qs=ds&form=CONVAJ&showconv=1#
- https://www.breachlock.com/resources/blog/benefits-of-phishing-simulations/
- https://www.caranddriver.com/auto-loans/a32799402/dealer-options/
- https://www.cbtnews.com/shifting-focus-making-your-dealerships-data-work-for-you/
- https://www.cdkglobal.com/sites/cdk4/files/PDFfiles/22-4000%20State%20of%20Cybersecurity%202022_Ebook_V9.pdf
- https://www.cisa.gov/sites/default/files/publications/Cyber%20Essentials%20Toolkit%202%2020200701.pdf
- https://www.cisco.com/c/en_in/products/security/email-security/what-is-phishing.html
- https://www.cisecurity.org/-/jssmedia/Project/cisecurity/cisecurity/data/media/files/uploads/2021/11/NIST-Cybersecurity-Framework-Policy-Template-Guide-v2111Online.pdf
- https://www.condorsecurity.ca/6-benefits-getting-security-audit/
- https://www.cpomagazine.com/cyber-security/kia-motors-america-suffers-a-20-million-suspected-doppelpaymer-ransomware-attack/
- https://www.crowdstrike.com/cybersecurity-101/endpoint-security/
- https://www.csoonline.com/article/514515/what-is-phishing-examples-types-and-techniques.html

- https://www.csoonline.com/article/570281/csos-ultimate-guide-to-security-and-privacy-laws-regulations-and-compliance.html
- https://www.deloitte.com/global/en/services/risk-advisory/blogs/physical-security-the-shift-in-perspective.html
- https://www.diligent.com/insights/business-continuity/bcp-maintenance/
- https://www.dnsstuff.com/vulnerability-and-patch-management
- https://www.eccouncil.org/cybersecurity-exchange/network-security/firewall-security-guide-concerns-capabilities-limitations/
- https://www.esecurityplanet.com/networks/patch-management-best-practices/
- https://www.exabeam.com/explainers/siem/incident-response-and-automation/
- https://www.exabeam.com/incident-response/incident-response-plan/
- https://www.exabeam.com/information-security/top-8-social-engineering-techniques-and-how-to-prevent-them-2022/
- https://www.fisherphillips.com/en/news-insights/auto-dealership-compliance-new-information-security-rules.html
- https://www.forbes.com/sites/forbesbusinesscouncil/2021/05/27/the-importance-of-a-strong-security-culture-and-how-to-build-one/
- https://www.forbes.com/sites/forbestechcouncil/2022/07/22/social-engineering-threats-and-mitigation/
- https://www.fortinet.com/blog/industry-trends/the-need-for-endpoint-security-isnt-going-away
- https://www.fortinet.com/resources/cyberglossary/what-is-siem
- https://www.frontiersin.org/articles/10.3389/fpubh.2021.788347/full
- https://www.ftc.gov/business-guidance/industry/automobiles
- https://www.ftc.gov/business-guidance/resources/ftc-safeguards-rule-what-your-business-needs-know
- https://www.ftc.gov/business-guidance/resources/ftcs-privacy-rule-auto-dealers-faqs
- https://www.ftc.gov/business-guidance/small-businesses/cybersecurity/basics
- https://www.ftc.gov/legal-library/browse/statutes/fair-credit-reporting-act
- https://www.ftc.gov/system/files/documents/plain-language/560a_data_breach_response_guide_for_business.pdf
- https://www.ibm.com/downloads/cas/JZ38L39E
- https://www.ibm.com/topics/pretexting
- https://www.ibm.com/topics/siem

- https://www.icaew.com/regulation/regulatory-news/2021-june/the-role-of-the-mlro-beyond-compliance
- https://www.ifrc.org/document/data-protection-overview-and-best-practices
- https://www.indeed.com/career-advice/career-development/centralized-management
- https://www.isaca.org/resources/isaca-journal/issues/2019/volume-2/how-to-increase-cybersecurity-awareness
- https://www.isaca.org/resources/news-and-trends/industry-news/2022/an-integrated-approach-to-security-audits
- https://www.liveabout.com/a-guide-to-dealership-structure-4082435
- https://www.loginradius.com/blog/identity/benefits-of-mfa/
- https://www.makeuseof.com/importance-cybersecurity-training-employees/
- https://www.mckinsey.com/~/media/mckinsey/industries/automotive%20and%20assembly/our%20insights/cybersecurity%20in%20automotive%20mastering%20the%20challenge/cybersecurity-in-automotive-mastering-the-challenge.pdf
- https://www.mckinsey.com/capabilities/risk-and-resilience/our-insights/the-consumer-data-opportunity-and-the-privacy-imperative
- https://www.mckinsey.com/industries/automotive-and-assembly/our-insights/as-dramatic-disruption-comes-to-automotive-showrooms-proactive-dealers-can-benefit-greatly#/
- https://www.mckinsey.com/industries/automotive-and-assembly/our-insights/cybersecurity-in-automotive-mastering-the-challenge
- https://www.mckinsey.com/industries/automotive-and-assembly/our-insights/the-race-for-cybersecurity-protecting-the-connected-car-in-the-era-of-new-regulation
- https://www.nada.org/index.php/safeguardsrule
- https://www.nerdwallet.com/article/small-business/cybersecurity-insurance
- https://www.npsa.gov.uk/security-culture
- https://www.pcisecuritystandards.org/
- https://www.pondurance.com/blog/ftc-safeguards-for-auto-dealerships/
- https://preparecenter.org/sites/default/files/handout3dataprotectionfaqs210618.pdf
- https://www.rapid7.com/fundamentals/security-awareness-training/
- https://www.regpacks.com/blog/secure-payment-processing/

- https://www.scmagazine.com/news/security-awareness/a-third-of-companies-dont-offer-cybersecurity-training-to-remote-workers
- https://www.securitymagazine.com/articles/98487-phishing-is-the-top-cybersecurity-threat-targeting-car-dealerships
- https://www.seyfarth.com/news-insights/ftc-begins-process-to-adopt-rules-for-new-car-dealer-advertising-and-sales.html
- https://www.tripwire.com/state-of-security/auto-industry-higher-risk-cyberattacks
- https://www.vistainfosec.com/blog/testing-the-business-continuity-plan/
- https://www.wardsauto.com/sites/wardsauto.com/files/uploads/2016/TheBigStory-Dealer-1016-2.pdf
- https://www2.deloitte.com/us/en/insights/topics/risk-management/consumer-data-privacy-strategies.html

INDEX

LEGISLATION SUMMARIES

- **California Consumer Privacy Act:** Imposes restrictions on personal information usage, requiring dealerships to notify consumers about data practices and allowing opt-out of data sharing.
- **Colorado Consumer Protection Act:** Facilitates pursuit of deceptive practices, increasing maximum violation penalties and enforcing consumer protection.
- **Hawaii SB418:** Encompasses broader reach for data protection without a private right of action; enforced by the Office of Consumer Protection.
- **Illinois SB 1624:** Requires breach notification to the attorney general for breaches involving at least five hundred Illinois residents.
- **Louisiana Database Security Breach Notification Law:** Expands personal information definition, mandates breach notice within sixty days, and enforces "reasonable security procedures."
- **Maine An Act to Protect the Privacy of Online Customer Information:** Applies to ISPs, protecting online customer data privacy.
- **Maryland Online Consumer Protection Act:** Modeled after CCPA, offering expanded consumer opt-out rights.
- **Massachusetts Act Relative to Consumer Data Privacy:** Stricter than CCPA, prohibits sharing with minors, allowing private right of action, effective 2023.
- **Mississippi Consumer Privacy Act:** Similar to CCPA, bill stalled in committee.
- **Nebraska LB757:** Requires reasonable security procedures and practices, including personal info safeguards.
- **Nevada SB 220:** Modeled after CCPA, applies to web site owners; no private right of action.
- **New Jersey A-4902:** Focuses on disclosure of personally identifiable information; applies to commercial web sites.
- **New Mexico Consumer Information Privacy Act:** Modeled after CCPA but broader scope; currently postponed indefinitely.
- **New York SB-S224:** Broader than CCPA, extends private right of action; potential for multiple lawsuits from consumers.

- **North Dakota House Bill 1485:** Prohibits disclosure without written consent; replaced by legislative study.
- **Ohio Data Protection Act:** Shields businesses from lawsuits, even after a security breach, with reasonable measures.
- **Oregon Consumer Information Protection Act:** Requires breach notification, covers "covered entities," reporting within ten days.
- **Rhode Island Consumer Privacy Protection Act:** Modeled after CCPA; pending further study.
- **Texas Identity Theft Enforcement and Protection Act:** Requires breach notifications within sixty days, with penalties, effective 2020.
- **Washington Privacy Act:** Modeled after CCPA and GDPR, no private right of action; in legislative process.

ABOUT THE AUTHOR

Born in Georgetown, Guyana, and educated across three countries—Guyana, Canada, and the USA—Brian Ramphal has risen as a pivotal tech entrepreneur and angel investor specializing in the automotive vertical. With a rich experience spanning twenty-five years, he has been vital in creating bespoke technology products and services for automotive OEMs, dealer groups, and franchise dealerships. His unparalleled understanding of the automotive vertical's intricacies is backed by a solid academic foundation in computer science and an MBA, further enriched by executive management cybersecurity training from MIT.

Brian's debut book, *Automotive Dealership Safeguard: Cybersecurity & Financial Compliance Guide,* is a meticulously crafted guide for franchise automotive dealerships across the US. With cybersecurity becoming an acute concern for dealerships—as evidenced by CDK Global's report highlighting 85 percent of dealerships ranking cybersecurity as a paramount operational area—the book aims to empower stakeholders with actionable strategies to mitigate risks.

By meticulously unraveling the anatomy of automotive cyberattacks, Brian doesn't merely spotlight vulnerabilities but transcends to offer robust solutions anchored in esteemed standards, such as ISO 21434 and the revered NIST frameworks. The book champions the imperativeness of relentless employee training in cybersecurity, directing readers toward the comprehensive automotive dealerships online training platform at <u>www.comply.law</u>.

This guide bestows automotive dealership owners, executives, professionals, and frontline employees with pragmatic acumen, from decrypting the intertwined challenges of cybersecurity and financial compliance to understanding the far-reaching ramifications of fortified data protection on business dynamics, financial health, and stakeholder trust. Brian's adeptness in articulating complex concepts, refined over years of mentoring at renowned institutions, renders the content approachable for both beginners and experts alike.

But for Brian, this book is just the commencement. He has architected a thriving learning hub at <u>www.comply.law</u>, inviting dealerships to immerse their workforce in a myriad of online training modules, encompassing everything from cybersecurity nuances to OSHA and HR regulatory compliance.

For those at the helm of dealerships, professionals eager to elevate their expertise, or the inquisitive minds intrigued by the synergy of technology and automobiles, Brian Ramphal's *Automotive Dealership Safeguard* beckons as a luminary guide illuminating the intricate maze of automotive cybersecurity and regulatory adherence.

Printed in the United States
by Baker & Taylor Publisher Services